To Marilyn,
Keep following
your Star!

Edward Chin

The
Wonder
of Words

The Wonder of Words

Book II

ONE-HUNDRED MORE WORDS AND PHRASES SHAPING HOW CHRISTIANS THINK AND LIVE

EDWARD CHINN

C.S.S. Publishing Co., Inc.

Lima, Ohio

THE WONDER OF WORDS: BOOK 2

Printed in the United States of America for
C.S.S. Publishing Company,
628 South Main Street, Lima, Ohio 45804
and
Forward Movement Publications,
412 Sycamore Street, Cincinnati, Ohio 45202

Library of Congress Cataloging-in-Publication Data

Chinn, Edward, 1931-
The wonder of words, book 2.

Bibliography: p.
1. Meditations. 2. Christian life — Anglican authors. I. Title. II. Title: Wonder of words.
BV4832.2.C5285 1987 242 86-28366
ISBN 0-89536-867-6
ISBN 0-88028-059-X (Forward Movement)

7824 / ISBN 0-89536-865-X PRINTED IN U.S.A.

Dedicated
to
KATHY, LINDA, AND STEPHEN
who taught me the
wonder of the word *father*

Contents

Preface

Mark Twain occasionally attended worship services at St. John's Episcopal Church in Hartford, Connecticut. The pastor of St. John's was the Reverend William Croswell Doane, later to become the first bishop of the Diocese of Albany, New York. One Sunday morning, Twain approached the pastor at the end of the service and said, "Dr. Doane, I enjoyed your sermon this morning. I welcomed it like an old friend. I have, you know, a book at home containing every word of it." Indignantly, Dr. Doane replied, "You have not!" Twain answered firmly, "I have so." "Well," said the pastor, "you send that book to me. I'd like to see it." "I'll send it," promised Twain. The following day he sent Dr. Doane an unabridged dictionary.

You can find every word of this second book about *The Wonder of Words* in the dictionary, just as Mark Twain found Dr. Doane's words there. As a matter of fact, many of the following pages started as I went to the dictionary to check etymologies and to discover the vivid pictures locked inside the history of common words. Other pages began when I came across a story (and sometimes a joke) that seemed to point me toward a certain word.

As I write these words, I am about to celebrate my twenty-fifth anniversary as the pastor of All Saints' Episcopal Church in the far northeast corner of the city of Philadelphia. I owe a great debt of gratitude to the men and women and children of this splendid congregation, with whom I have shared the contents of these pages through sermons and newsletters. Over the years the kindness, patience, and encouragement of these folk have defined, for me, the meaning of that word which Jesus chose for his companions, when he said, "I have called you *friends.*" (John 15:15)

I want to acknowledge and thank Mrs. Cary (Dodie) Rush, a member of All Saints' Church, for her invaluable help in proofreading the original manuscript and the computer print-out of this book. May the following pages renew your awareness of the wonder of words!

Edward Chinn

1

Adam

Adam and Eve had an ideal marriage. He didn't have to hear about all the men she could have married — and she didn't have to hear about the way his mother cooked. It is said that after Adam and Eve were expelled from the Garden of Eden, Adam once took a walk with his sons, Cain and Abel. Cain noticed the beautiful Garden of Eden and said, "Father, that's a beautiful place. Why don't we live there?" "Son," Adam replied, "we used to live there until your mother ate us out of house and home!"

Although we are accustomed to thinking of *Adam* as the personal name of a particular historical character, the term is actually a collective noun which stands for all men. This is what the surprising grammatical movement from the singular to the plural implies, in the words of God the Creator in this text: "Let us make man (Adam) in our image . . . and let them have dominion . . ." (Genesis 1:26)

Our human story is written in the drama of the two Adams. The first Adam is of the earth. In Hebrew, the word for man (Adam) comes from the word for ground (adamah). As we read the story of Adam in chapters two and three of the Book of Genesis, we are reading "moral ideas in the form of a story." (Gregory of Nyssa) Adam misused the gift of freedom, failed to trust God, rebelled against his command, and became enslaved by a sense of inadequacy, insecurity, and anxiety. (Genesis 3:10)

The second Adam is from heaven. He is the Word or Son of God who "became flesh and dwelt among us, full of grace and truth." (John 1:14) In the first Adam, man said his defiant, "No," to God. In the second Adam (Christ), God's divine, "Yes," has at last sounded, affirming the dignity and destiny of humanity. As John Henry Newman wrote: "O loving wisdom of our God! When all was sin and shame, a second Adam to the fight and to the rescue came."

2

Affirm

Jesus once told a story about a woman who kept nagging a greedy and unjust judge until his resistance was worn down, and he finally gave her what she wanted. (Luke 18:1-8) In that parable, Jesus contrasted a mean judge to our loving heavenly Father, who is anxious to give us his good gifts. In another instance, Jesus compared God's willingness to give, to the willingness of an earthly parent: "You know how to give good things to your children. How much more, then, will your Father in heaven give good things to those who ask him." (Matthew 7:11) If the secret of receiving God's good gifts is to ask for them, then we'd better learn just how Jesus wants us to ask! He has told us how to do it! This is what he said: "Everything you ask and pray for, believe that you have it already and it will be yours." (Mark 11:24, The Jerusalem Bible)

What did Jesus mean by the phrase, "Believe that you have it already"? He meant for you to use your God-given power of sanctified imagination! See, in your mind's eye, God is now giving you his good gifts. Unfortunately, many people, in prayer, do just the opposite of what Jesus recommended. They concentrate on the problem instead of visualizing the positive desired effects. Jesus calls us to practice the Prayer of Affirmation. In the Greek text of Jesus' words, in Mark 11:24, the verb "believe" is in the present tense, implying continuous action: "Keep on believing"! This is called "The Prayer of Affirmation" because an affirmation is a positive statement, an assertion of truth, a declaration made in trust that the good Lord is already giving us his good gifts. The word *affirm* comes from two Latin words, "ad" (to) and "firmare" (to strengthen). Prayer is not overcoming God's reluctance. It is laying hold affirmatively on his willingness to give good gifts to his earthly children. Modern medicine, in its use of "guided imagery," is only now catching up to Jesus.

3

Alone

"No man is an island," wrote the seventeenth century Anglican priest, John Donne. Without denying the validity of that insight, we need to see the opposite is also true. Spanish philosopher Ortega y Gasset wrote: "Each man is an island in that he lives and dies in the solitude of his own consciousness." Each of us is alone, shut up in his own skin and thoughts. The word *alone* comes from two medieval English words: "al" (all) and "one" (one). To be alone is to be all by one's self, to be apart from other persons and things. To be physically alone is solitude. To be psychologically alone is loneliness. The man who wrote Psalm 102 experienced loneliness: "I am like a pelican in the desert, like an owl in abandoned ruins. I lie awake; I am like a lonely bird on a housetop." (Psalm 102:6-7) The loneliness of displacement is pictured by a water bird, a pelican, in the wilderness. That bird is removed from where it feels at home. The loneliness of detachment is seen in the owl clinging, in self-chosen isolation, to the ruins of the past. The loneliness of disesteem is imaged in the insignificance of a solitary bird perched on a roof.

In Jesus' life we see a man who coped successfully with loneliness. He discovered loneliness: "I will be left alone. But I am not really alone, because the Father is with me." (John 16:32) He coped with loneliness by turning to faith. Secondly, Jesus disliked loneliness. While he enjoyed the solitude of early morning hours, he combated loneliness by selecting twelve companions: "I have chosen you to be with me," he told them. (Mark 3:14) He coped by establishing a fellowship of believers, a fellowship to which we can turn today at the local church. Thirdly, Jesus dealt with loneliness by turning to the needs of other persons, like the man whose disease isolated him from society: "Jesus was filled with pity, and reached out and touched him." (Mark 1:41) Fourthly, Jesus drove out loneliness by realizing he had a dominating life purpose, a star to follow: "I was born and came into the world for this one purpose, to speak about the truth." (John 18:37)

4

Amateur

In a certain haunted castle, a ghost was said to appear only once in every 100 years. A group of amateur photographers was determined to get a picture of the ghost. One of the amateur photographers was chosen by the others to take the picture. He went to the castle and sat in the darkness until midnight, when the apparition became visible. The ghost turned out to be friendly and agreed to pose for a snapshot. The amateur photographer was overjoyed, popped a bulb into his camera, and took the picture. Then he dashed to his studio, developed the negative, and groaned with disappointment. It was underexposed and nearly blank. The amateur photographers drew the following moral from the experience: "The spirit was willing, but the flash was weak"!

The word amateur is often used in the sense of something done poorly by an unskilled person. Actually, the word *amateur* comes from the Latin "amare" (to love). An amateur is, in this root sense, a person who does something for the sheer love of doing it, not simply for money. Sir Winston Churchill, for example, was called an "amateur painter," even though his works had genuine artistic merit. He was an "amateur" because he worked for the sheer love of painting. In the first book of Plato's *Republic,* Socrates insisted on the difference between the true artist (in any field) who practices his art (medicine, for example) for the sake of its true object (in the case of medicine, health) and the artist who practices his art "as a moneymaker." Of course, it is right the doctor should earn his fee. However, the earning of the fee must not be the directing motive of his practice. Every *amateur* reminds us you can buy a man's time, physical presence at a given place, and skilled motions per hour, but you can't buy his enthusiasm, initiative, loyalty, and the devotion of heart. These flow naturally from the man who loves what he is doing.

5

Ancestors

Unless some things are carried from the past into the future, there will be no future worth having. That's what the Bible means when it tells us about Joseph's dying words: "And Joseph made his people swear an oath, 'When God remembers you with kindness, be sure to take my bones from here.' " (Genesis 50:25) Centuries later, when the Hebrews escaped from Egypt, the narrative says, "Moses took the bones of Joseph with him." (Exodus 13:19)

One thing we need to carry from the past into the future is a respect for the *ancestors* we have. That's how Will Rogers felt. When a snobbish member of a prominent New England family boasted to him that her ancestors came over in the Mayflower, Will, who was proud of his Indian blood, replied, "Yes, and my ancestors were here to meet them!" Among your ancestors are the noblest souls of our race: Moses, Plato, Mary, and Paul, and, above all, Jesus of Nazareth.

Another thing we need to carry from the past into the future is a respect for the ancestors we are. T.S. Eliot called this our "solicitude for the unborn." Educator John Dewey put it this way: "The best we can accomplish for posterity is to transmit unimpaired and with some increment of meaning the environment that makes it possible to maintain the habits of decent and refined life." When a time capsule was buried in Long Island during the 1939 World's Fair in New York, the Bible was the only full-size book included. Authorities explained: "The Holy Bible, of all the books familiar to us today, will most likely survive through the ages. Therefore, the Bible that we placed in the Time Capsule will be sort of a connecting link between the past, the present, and the future." That's a modern version of the old Bible story about carrying Joseph's bones to Canaan. Unless some things are carried from the past into the future, there'll be no future worth having!

6

Atonement

Atonement is the word Christians use to sum up what Jesus' death means to them. That word was invented by William Tyndale, the fifteenth century translator of the Bible into English. Tyndale sought an English equivalent for the Old Testament Hebrew root "kaphar" and the New Testament Greek word "katallage." Finding none, he created a new word from the preposition "at" and the word "one." Atonement is the healing or mending of a hurt or broken relationship. If we would pronounce that word as at-one-ment, we would be constantly reminded of its basic meaning.

Take a human example: a man has wronged his wife. How will he attempt to make things at one again? He could apologize for the past. He could make promises to do better in the future. He could offer a present to her. One thing, however, becomes clear. While the offender can *make* the separation, he cannot *heal* the separation. *At-one-ment* can take place only if the person offended maintains the standards, absorbs the hurt, and reaches out in love.

Now lift that personal transaction to the divine level. How can mankind bridge the separation from God which sin has caused? Like the erring husband, mankind has confessed past wrongs, promised future amendment of life, and tried offering gifts (sacrifices) to God. "Yom Kippur," the Jewish Day of Atonement, was the day, in ancient times, when the high priest offered a sacrifice to God in the Jewish Temple to make atonement. However, just as the human efforts of the offender cannot create atonement, neither can mankind's efforts create atonement with God. At-one-ment can only take place when God takes the initiative, absorbs the hurt, reaches out in love, and bridges the gap. Christians see divine initiative in the life, death, and resurrection of Jesus. That's why St. Paul wrote: "We joy in God through our Lord Jesus Christ who has given us the atonement." (Romans 5:11)

7
Authority

"By what authority are you acting like this?" was the question posed to Jesus by the religious leaders. (Mark 11:27) This question of authority, in matters of religion, is at the basis of most of our controversies in the church today. The word *authority* comes from the Latin word "auctoritas," which, in turn, comes from the word "auctor," meaning one who causes to grow. There are two forms of authority: external and internal. External authority is signified by the Latin word "imperium," and refers to the right to be obeyed. This external authority is attached to an office, such as policeman, bishop, emperor. The disciples of Jesus had been brought up to think of authority in terms of power. "In the world," said Jesus, "the recognized rulers lord it over their subjects, and their great men make them feel the weight of authority." (Mark 10:42) When Jesus lived, the clearest example of external authority was in the Roman system, with its headquarters in Rome. Today there are Christians who find their religious authority in the external imperium of the church, or a certain leader, or the Bible. Yet the church has erred in morals, in opposing the discoveries of science, and in its witness to the Word of God. The chosen leader can be wrong. The same Bible is claimed and appealed to by contradictory groups.

Internal authority is signified by the Latin word "auctoritas," and refers to the weight of evidence, experience, or example. Such internal authority is seen in that of a scientist, a musician, or a saint. Jesus revolutionized the disciples' concept of authority when he directed their attention to the Roman system of external authority, and then said: "That is not the way with you; whoever wants to be great must be your servant." (Mark 10:43) People recognized this inherent authority in Jesus when they said about him: "He speaks with authority." (Mark 1:27) Jesus' authority rested on three factors. He himself was submissive to the authority of God. (John 8:28) He saw that real authority came from serving people. (Mark 10:45) He was sensitive in his dealing with people, so sensitive folk remembered Isaiah's words: "He will not snap off the broken reed, nor snuff out the smouldering wick." (Matthew 12:20)

8

Babies

In the early 1830's, in France, a schoolmaster wrote these words in his rollbook, after the name of one of his pupils: "He is the smallest, the meekest, the most unpromising boy in my class." Half a century later, a popular election was held, in France, to determine who was the greatest Frenchman. By popular vote, that meekest, smallest, most unpromising boy was voted to be the greatest Frenchman. The boy who grew into a national hero was Louis Pasteur, the founder of modern medicine. Before his death at age seventy-three, a national holiday was declared in his honor. He was too old and weak to attend the ceremony in Paris, so he sent a message to be read by his son. The message read: "The future belongs not to the conquerors but to the saviours of the world."

If you could go back to the city of Rome on the night Jesus was born, imagine how important the Roman conquerors would appear to be. Their battles paved the way for the Roman Empire's vast rule. In contrast to those battles, how insignificant, in the scale of things, would appear a tiny baby, born in the obscure village of Bethlehem on the fringe of the Empire. Even so, nearly 2,000 years later, we sing not about Rome, but about Bethlehem: "Yet in thy dark streets shineth the everlasting light; The hopes and fears of all the years are met in thee tonight." *Babies* can outweigh battles!

That means things are never as hopeless as they look. In 1809 Napoleon was on the march and all Europe was discouraged. But consider the babies born in 1809: Abraham Lincoln, Alfred Lord Tennyson, Charles Darwin, Edgar Allan Poe, Oliver Wendell Holmes, Felix Mendelssohn. History has written "Futile" across the *battles* of 1809. History is still vibrating from the impact of the *babies* of 1809. Ponder the words of Carl Sandburg: "A baby is God's opinion that life should go on."

9

Ballot

At election time, we enter the polling booth to choose a candidate, by using a pencil or pulling a lever to mark a ballot. The word *ballot* comes from the Italian word "ballotta," meaning little ball. In ancient Rome and Greece, voting was done by means of little balls which the voter deposited in a receptacle. If he favored the candidate, he cast a white ball; if he opposed the person, he dropped in a black ball. From that custom we get the verb "to blackball," meaning to exclude from membership in an organization.

People vote in ways other than using pencils, pulling levers, or dropping balls. The most common and sincere way you vote is with your feet! Our nation is a nation of immigrants who voted with their feet as they walked down gangplanks or stepped from airplanes onto the soil of America.

You vote with your feet when you go to church. People can talk a great deal about the importance of the church. They can discuss, for hours, how important it is to support positive, practical religion. People can say they want their children trained in an awareness of the religious dimension of life. Our real choices and our true values, however, show up not just in our talk, but in our walk. You vote for the church or the synagogue and for the spiritual interpretation of life when you walk into your house of worship each week. Your presence there is a ringing affirmation that you vote for America to be "one nation under God."

You vote with your feet whenever you choose to follow a particular course of action. Ponder the roads you've chosen to walk and the doors you've elected to enter, and you'll see what a difference those choices have made in your life. The man who collected proverbs, in the Bible, captured this truth about the human being, when he wrote these words: "He speaketh with his feet." (Proverbs 6:13)

10

Branded

Once upon a time, two brothers were convicted of stealing sheep. Each brother was *branded* on the forehead with the letters *ST* for "sheep thief." One brother was unable to bear the stigma, so he moved to a foreign land. People constantly asked him about those stange letters on his brow. He wandered restlessly and, finally, full of bitterness, died and was buried in a forgotten grave. The other brother said to himself: "I can't run away from the fact that I stole sheep. I will stay here and win back the respect of my neighbors and myself." As the years passed, this brother built a reputation for integrity. Many times he turned the pages of his Bible to words found in the sixty-second chapter of Isaiah: "You will be called by a new name." Years later, a stranger saw this old man with the letters branded on his forehead. When the stranger inquired what they meant, a townsman replied, "It's so long ago that I forget the details, but I think the letters are an abbreviation for 'saint'."

Consider how often human beings have been branded as worthless by recent writers, dramatists, and philosophers. Albert Camus, the French writer, pictured man as "Sisyphus," after a character in a Greek legend who had the meaningless job of pushing a stone uphill again and again. Desmond Morris wrote a book about man called *The Naked Ape.* Albert Szent-Gyorgi, a marine biologist, called his book about man *The Crazy Ape.* No wonder many people today ask whether life has any meaning, and whether human beings have any value! They need to hear that encouraging promise of the Bible: "You will be called by a new name." The biblical writers address you as "Image of God" (Genesis 1:27); "Master of creation" (Psalm 8:6); "The World's Seasoning" (Matthew 5:13); "The World's Light" (Matthew 5:14); "God's coworker" (1 Corinthians 3:9); "God's Child" (1 John 3:1). God made you greater than any problem you face!

11

Breath

"Closer is He than breathing, and nearer than hands and feet," wrote Alfred Lord Tennyson about God. When we think of God and of ourselves "in the same breath," then we are breathing with God, thinking in unison with him. When we ponder how human beings are made, marred, and made again, we notice the common theme running through these three events is this matter of *breath*.

First, man is made by God. In the second, and older, creation story in Genesis, God is pictured shaping man as a potter shapes a vessel out of clay. "Then the Lord God formed man of dust from the ground, and breathed into his nostrils the breath of life; and man became a living being." (Genesis 2:7) The word *breath* here stands for both the physical and the spiritual. That double meaning can be found in our English word "inspiration," meaning to breathe in.

Second, man, who has been made by God, has been marred by life. If you remember how the death of Jesus affected his disciples, you have a case study of how our lives get broken. Shocked by the sad, unexpected turn of events, they had the breath knocked out of them. Spent and exhausted, running away from Calvary, they were out of breath. Silenced by a hostile world, they saved their breath, because no one cared to listen.

Third, man can be made over again. When those fearful disciples hid behind locked doors, on the first day of a new week after Jesus died, he appeared among them in that upstairs room, greeted them with his characteristic word "Shalom," showed them his scars, and "then he breathed on them, saying 'Receive holy breath (spirit)'." (John 20:22) By that wonderfully-acted parable, Jesus recalled the original creation, and re-created them by imparting, to them (and to us), his own life-breath, his own spiritual energy, to carry on his work in his world.

12

Bridge Builders

In A.D. 1191, Pope Clement III approved a new guild. Its members included nobles, clergy, and artisans. The work of the guild consisted of clearing dangerous roads for pilgrims and building bridges over rivers and chasms. Members of the guild wore clothing that carried a picture of two things: a cross and a bridge. The guild was called "fratres pontifices," the *bridge-building brothers.* The guild of medieval bridge builders has long ceased to exist; yet, in a figurative sense, all men of good will are bridge builders. An Episcopal priest, Dr. Joseph Fort Newton, once commented: "People are lonely because they build walls instead of bridges."

When a bridge is being planned, engineers must take into account three loads the bridge will have to bear: the dead load, the live load, and the wind load. The dead load is the bridge itself. In human terms, this refers to the human being who is serving as a bridge between people. To leaders of the congregation in the city of Ephesus who were doing that kind of work, St. Paul advised, "Be careful about your own spiritual life."

The live load which must be considered in bridge building is the traffic that crosses the bridge. In human terms, this refers to the people for whom you are the mediator. People in Argentina and Chile, for example, were poised for war in 1899, when an Argentine bishop appealed for peace. A Chilean bishop took up his cause and the dispute was submitted to King Edward VII whose decision settled the quarrel. The unused guns from both countries were melted down to be used in a colossal statue of Christ, erected on a mountain range between the two countries.

The wind load is the pressure of the wind on the structure of the bridge. In human terms, this refers to the adversities bridge builders face. Such adversity makes us tighten up, adding to the strain. The French philosopher, Gabriel Marcel, put his finger on the answer to this wind load when he spoke about "the secret affinity between hope and relaxation."

13

Cabbage Patch Kids

Cabbage Patch Kids are dolls invented by Xavier Roberts. They are said to come from "BabyLand General Hospital" in Cleveland, Georgia. According to the legend of the Cabbage Patch Kids, a young boy named Xavier stumbled upon an enchanted Cabbage Patch. There he discovered little people who called themselves Cabbage Patch Kids. Xavier Roberts has turned that idea and his original $300 of materials into a multi-million dollar corporation. People wait in lines, all night, in front of stores that have a supply of these dolls, so they can buy one for their children.

Christians can find four lessons from these Cabbage Patch Kids. First, like those dolls, we are adopted. With each doll comes an individualized birth certificate and adoption papers. In the New Testament, the metaphor of adoption is used to describe God's unearned kindness to us, expressed in Jesus of Nazareth. As the only natural Son of God, Jesus shares with us his intimate relationship with God his Father. "You received the Spirit of adoption by whom we cry, 'Abba, Father'." (Romans 8:15)

Second, like those dolls, we now belong to a family. "You are now . . . members of the family of God," wrote St. Paul. (Ephesians 2:19) The language of our faith is derived from the family circle: God is our father; the church is our mother; Christ is our elder brother; and the altar in the church is our family table.

Third, like those dolls, we are comforted by one who loves us with a mother's love. Through the prophet Isaiah, God spoke, using feminine imagery to tell of his care: "As a mother comforts her son, so will I comfort you." (Isaiah 66:13)

Fourth, like those dolls, we are lovingly dressed. When the erring son returned home in Jesus' parable about the loving Father, "the father called to his servants. 'Hurry!' he said. 'Bring the best robe and put it on him'." (Luke 15:22) By being dressed in that robe, the son was not only forgiven, but was received with honor. Reflecting on the parable, St. Paul wrote: "You were baptized into union with Christ, and now you are clothed, so to speak, with the life of Christ himself." (Galatians 3:27)

14

Caesar

In Las Vegas there was an old Christian saint, named Sam, who was approaching his eightieth birthday. Sam decided to look his best on the big day. He bought a hair piece, got silicone shots for his cheeks, had his double chin removed by plastic surgery, worked out at a gym, and bought a new suit. At the Las Vegas church he attended, Sam met a good-looking widow who was forty years old. He invited her to have dinner with him at Caesar's Palace, one of the Las Vegas casinos. He picked her up in his new sports car, drove her to the casino, escorted her to the door, when a bolt of lightning struck and killed him. In the hereafter, Sam cried, "Lord, why me?" And the Lord answered, "Sam? I'm sorry. I didn't recognize you."

Over nineteen hundred years ago there was another Caesar's Palace in Rome. When St. Paul wrote his letter to the Christians in Philippi, he closed with these words: "All the other Christians here want to be remembered to you, especially those who work in Caesar's Palace." (Philippians 4:22, The Living Bible) Caesar's Palace (or "Caesar's household" in other translations) was a general term for those who worked in the imperial civil service. *Caesar* was a title which came from the family name of Julius Caesar, who ruled Rome from 49 to 44 B.C. Caesar's nephew and adopted son, Octavian, took his uncle's name (Caesar) and also the title Augustus. The next four Roman Emperors — Tiberius, Caligula, Claudius, and Nero — claimed the name Caesar. Because of its association with the Emperor, the family name became a title. During the period of the Byzantine Empire, anyone chosen as a ruler of a country under the Empire might be called Caesar. The word passed into the Russian language as czar and into German as Kaiser. When a child is born by means of an operation through the abdominal and uterine walls, it is known as a Caesarean section because Julius Caesar is said to have been born in this way.

15

Carpenter

"I can't figure this out," complained a little boy. He was stuck on a homework problem in arithmetic. His father stooped down beside him and asked him to read the problem. The boy picked up his composition book and read, "If a carpenter was paid $3 a day, how much did he earn in four days?" The father scratched his head and said, "A carpenter making $3 a day? No wonder you can't figure it out! That's not arithmetic. That's ancient history."

The word *carpenter* comes from the Latin word "carpentarius," meaning a carriage maker. During the Middle Ages, the carpenter's guild in England adopted Christ's words, "I am the door," as their guild motto. As they built a door, they worked the sign of the cross into it by using a long upright center board and a short horizontal board. Four wooden panels filled in the spaces around the cross. The carpenters of England did this in honor of the Carpenter of Nazareth. Once, when Jesus visited his hometown of Nazareth, his neighbors whispered to each other, "Is not this the carpenter, the son of Mary?" (Mark 6:3)

What did Jesus learn from those years he spent as a carpenter? First, Jesus learned there are hidden possibilities in logs. In that unlikely-looking piece of wood was the potential for a plow, or a yoke, or a chair. No wonder he could, in later years, see a possible follower in a fisherman, a talented evangelist in a tax collector, and the first preacher of the Resurrection in a former prostitute. Second, Jesus learned that hours of patient labor were necessary to transform a tree into a table, and a branch into a bowl. That patience came in handy later on, as he undertook the painstaking task of turning Simon into Peter and Saul into Paul. Third, Jesus learned the satisfaction of seeing a job through to the end. Many times he must have run his hand over a smooth piece of wood and said, "It is finished." Maybe he had that in mind on Good Friday, when he, who had worked with wood and nails, was executed on two pieces of wood with nails in his hands.

16

Catharsis

The scientific study of human anatomy is a very recent development. Ancient doctors refused to cut into a corpse because they feared the ghost of the deceased. This fear promoted a "respect for the dead," which was expressed in English law by a statute prohibiting surgeons from practicing dissection. At the same time, however, advances in the field of medicine created a great demand for anatomical subjects. Professional grave robbers dug up bodies and sold them to physicians at high prices. Many a doctor, in earlier generations, dissected only one body in his lifetime. Of course, he would prize that skeleton highly and be reluctant to get rid of it. But public opinion made it dangerous for the doctor to keep it where it might be found. Therefore, the doctor hung his prize possession in some dark corner, where visitors would not see it. From this practice came the expression "a skeleton in the closet," which stands for some secret source of embarrassment, shame, or guilt.

Our sins and their guilt are skeletons in our psychological closets. The season of Lent recognizes this and calls for spiritual *catharsis*. That word comes from the Greek verb "kathairein," meaning to cleanse or purge. In the medical field, the word is used for the discharging of impurities. Aristotle used the word *catharsis* to describe how drama provided an outlet for our emotions. Guilt over those "skeletons in the closet" makes itself known by gossip, hypercriticism, overwork, illness, addiction, and an unconscious desire for punishment. As Shakespeare said, "The mind of guilt is full of scorpions." The Lenten season prescribes for us the *catharsis* of confession to God. The Bible puts it this way: "If we confess our sins to God . . . he will forgive us our sins and purify ("katharsis") us from all our wrongdoing." (1 John 1:9)

17

Christopher

In a kingdom long ago and far away, near the middle of the third century, there was a giant of a man named Reprobus. Reprobus made a vow he would serve the greatest king in the world. First he entered the service of the King of Canaan. But when Reprobus learned that the king feared the Devil, he sought out Satan and served him. However, he soon learned the Devil feared a king called Christ, so he went in search of Christ. On the way, he met a hermit who told him he could serve Christ best by doing well the kind of work for which he was best suited. Reprobus became a ferryman who carried on his broad shoulders any traveler who wished to cross a nearby bridgeless river. One stormy night a little child asked to be take across. Reprobus lifted him up and put him on his shoulder. With each step he took through the water, the child seemed to grow heavier. When he set the child down on the other side, Reprobus remarked, "Child, I felt as though I were carrying the burden of the world!" To this the child replied, "Thou hast indeed borne upon thy back the burden of the world and him who created it." Then Reprobus recognized that the child was Christ, the king he sought.

Reprobus' name was changed to Christopher, meaning Christ bearer. That name comes from two Greek words, "Christos" (Christ) and "pherein" (to bear). Every Christian is Christopher. To us, Christ says, "Thou hast indeed borne the burden of the world." That burden is the wild, untamed, chaotic elements of the world. "In the beginning," says Scripture, "God began to create . . . and the earth was without form." (Genesis 1:1-2) Since then, God has gradually extended his kingly rule over that primeval chaos. Chaos is one of God's ancient enemies along with sin, sickness, and death. "For Christ must rule until God defeats all enemies and puts them under his feet." (1 Corinthians 15:25) Not only, however, do we bear the burden of that chaos; we are also bearers of him who created the world and calls us to be co-workers with him for the world's good.

18

Consequences

"Of course, God will forgive me; that's his business!" Those flippant words were written by the nineteenth century German author, Heinrich Heine. Such a statement reveals a lack of understanding about the seriousness of sin. Where do sins go after they are committed? They go out into the world as evil consequences. *Consequence* comes from the Latin term "consequi," meaning to follow after. A consequence is a result that follows after an action, an effect flowing from a cause.

First, consider the consequences of sin for King David. "One evening David got up from his couch and, as he walked about on the roof of the palace, he saw from there a woman bathing, and she was very beautiful." (2 Samuel 11:2, NEB) The woman was Bathsheba, the wife of Uriah, an outstanding warrior. When Bathsheba became pregnant by David, he tried to get Uriah to spend a night home with his wife, but failed. David then told his general, Joab, to place Uriah in the front line of fighting where he would be killed. When Uriah was dead, David married Bathsheba. Later, the prophet Nathan confronted David with his crime. "David said to Nathan, 'I have sinned against the Lord.' Nathan answered him, 'The Lord has laid on another the consequences of your sin.' " (2 Samuel 12:13, NEB) The consequences of David's sin flowed out into the lives of Bathsheba, her child, Joab, and Uriah.

Second, consider the consequences of sin for others. For instance, Almeda Adams was the blind author of a book called "Seeing Europe Through Sightless Eyes." How did she become blind? When she was a few days old, a physician who was drunk used too strong a solution of silver nitrate on her eyes. The consequences of his sin were laid on her.

Third, consider the consequences of sin for God. Isaiah of Babylon pictured the perfect servant of God, whose suffering and death brought men to the knowledge of God. "The Lord laid upon him the guilt of us all." (Isaiah 52:6) In Jesus, we see that God is not an indifferent spectator of the world's pain, but an active participant who bears, in himself, the consequences of our sins.

19

Crazy

A little boy was confined to his house one rainy Sunday afternoon. He began to pester his father who wanted to take a nap. The father said, "Go away, son. Daddy's sleepy. Find something to play with." The boy whined, "I got nothing to play with." The father got up from the couch, picked up the Sunday newspaper, and found a large map of the world printed on one of the pages. He took a pair of scissors, cut the map out, and then cut it into many irregular shapes like a jigsaw puzzle. He told his son to put the map together, then turned over on the couch for a good nap. Ten minutes later the little boy was tapping his father's shoulder, saying "I'm all done." Sure enough, every piece of the map of the world had been fitted together perfectly. The father asked, "Son, how did you do that so quickly?" "It was easy, Daddy," the boy replied. "There's a picture of a man on the other side of the page. So I worked to put the man together. When I got the man right, the world turned out right, too."

"This is a crazy world," we sometimes say. The word *crazy* comes from the Swedish word "krasa," meaning cracked or broken. Just as the map of the world was broken up into little pieces, so lives get shattered like Humpty-Dumpty in the nursery rhyme. This brokenness in human nature is what the Christian church means by the word "sin." Note this important distinction: before "sin" is an act expressed in a person's thinking or talking or doing, "sin" is a fact, an essential state of brokenness in human nature. The real problem the Christian message is aimed at is not the moral problem of sins (plural); it is the metaphysical problem of sin (singular) as brokenness, craziness, separation from our true self (producing guilt), from other people (producing loneliness), and from reality or God (producing psychological emptiness and boredom).

20

Cross

Jesus transformed the *cross* from a revolting sight to a beloved symbol. That transformation is one of the marvels of history. The cross of Jesus has a three-fold message for you. First, the cross says, "You are loved by God." The positive meaning of the cross comes from the person of Jesus. If Jesus were only a good man, then his death would have been only another example of brave martyrdom. However, if you see, in the human life of Jesus, the personal presence and the loving power of God, then you see, in the crucified Jesus, the graphic expression that God's power is the persuasive and appealing power of unconquerable good will — love!

Second, the cross says, "You have been bought with a price." Some years ago, a former Archbishop of Canterbury, William Temple, was asked to speak on the meaning of the cross. The Archbishop chose two texts from the Bible. The first text was from the creation poem: "And God said, 'Let there be light,' and there was light." The second text was from the story of Jesus as he prayed in the Garden of Gethsemane, on the evening before he was crucified: "His sweat became like great drops of blood." The Archbishop pointed out the ease with which God created the universe and the painful cost he paid to re-create human nature. The cross is neither a sacrifice to the devil, nor a sacrifice to God. It is a sacrifice by God.

Third, the cross says, "You have a mission." Christian people are called to be "agents of the possible." The cross tells us we are sent on a mission to help men and women realize all the beautiful possibilities God has built into human life. Even when life has been spoiled and those possibilities have been crucified, dead, and buried, the empty cross tells us that every end is a new beginning!

21

Death and Resurrection

A little boy went to a doctor for a throat checkup and noticed a religious medal hanging from the doctor's neck. "What's that for?" he asked. "Oh, that's to remind me that I'm going to heaven," the doctor replied. "Wouldn't you like to go to heaven?" "Sure," the boy answered. "Well, now, what do you think we must do to get there?" the doctor questioned. "We must die," the boy responded. "Ah, yes, of course," the doctor smiled, "but what must we do before that?" The boy pondered and then said, "We must get sick and send for you."

That little boy didn't have much confidence in the doctor's healing ability, but he did recognize an important principle: unless you "die" to a lower existence, you cannot be "resurrected" to a higher level. For example, the plant says to the chemicals and moisture in the soil, "Unless you die to your lower existence, you cannot live in my kingdom." Likewise before the plant can live in the animal, it must be torn up from its roots and die. The animal says to the plant, "Unless you die to yourself, you cannot rise to my kingdom." When man, in turn, takes chemicals, plants, and animals into his nature, he says to them, "Unless you die to your present life, you cannot be resurrected in me."

Jesus demonstrated this death-resurrection principle. "Unless a grain of wheat falls into the earth and dies," he said, "it remains a single grain." By his *death and resurrection* Jesus transformed the tomb into a womb; the place of endings has become the place of new beginnings. If a person or a church is to live successfully, there must be a series of changes, of deaths and resurrections, to adapt to the changing environment. The dinosaur refused to change. The dinosaur is extinct. Isn't that what Jesus meant when he said, unless we are continually born anew, we cannot rise to God's Kingdom?

22

Defeat

"In love's service, only the wounded can serve," wrote Thornton Wilder in a three-minute play inspired by the biblical story about the Pool of Bethesda. The play is about a doctor who suffers from an incurable wound. He waits with other sick people at the Pool. He hopes to be healed by being the first to get into the water after an angel stirs it. However, the angel says to him: "Draw back, physician; healing is not for thee. Without your wound, where would your power be? It is your very sorrow that puts kindness in your face and makes your low voice tremble into the hearts of men. The angels themselves cannot heal the wretched as can one human being broken on the wheel of life. In love's service, only the wounded can serve."

The doctor, like the apostle Paul, was defeated in his quest for release from this thorn in the flesh. (2 Corinthians 12:8-9) That story reminded me of a chapter in a book of Methodist pastor, Charles L. Allen. The chapter is titled "Defeats May Be Your Greatest Blessings." First, defeats can make you more receptive. Thirty-five centuries ago, Moses was raised in the lap of Egyptian luxury, but life really started for him when he was forty years old. He murdered an Eygptian and ran away, a defeated man. *Defeat,* however, made him more receptive to God's voice. Second, defeat can make you more resourceful. A man felt financially defeated when he saw the land he had bought in Florida was filled with rattlesnakes. Defeat made him more resurceful. He opened a "Rattlesnake Farm" and sold the snakes' meat, skins and poison. Third, defeat can make you more redemptive. To redeem means to liberate by paying a price. When we pay the price to handle defeat well, we become "wounded healers" who help other persons to be set free from their fears and their failures.

23

Disappointment

"Yes," said the old man, "I've had some terrible disappointments, but none stands out over the years like the one that came to me when I was a boy. I crawled under a tent to see a circus and discovered it was a revival meeting!" None of us gets far into our life journey without some bitter, soul-searching disappointment. The word *disappointment* comes from two Old French words: "dis" (separated) and "appointer" (to resolve to do something). Disappointment is the frustration, the unfulfillment of some expectation or intention. Moses wanted to enter the Promised Land to which he had led his people, but that hope was disappointed. King David wanted to build the great Temple in Jerusalem, but that dream was frustrated. Paul the Apostle planned to go to Spain (Romans 15:24), but he ended up in a jail cell in Rome. Humanity is a shore strewn with the wrecks of disappointed hopes.

What can we do when things don't work out? First, we can check for a message. During one of his missionary journeys, Paul wanted very much to go into the province of Bithynia in Asia Minor, "but the Spirit of Jesus did not allow them." (Acts 16:7) Disappointed, Paul traveled instead to Troas, a seaport on the Aegean Sea, where he found the message to carry Christianity out of Asia into Europe. In his disappointment, Paul found God's appointment for a new experience. Second, we can change our outlook. In bitter disappointment over the loss of their cotton harvest to the boll weevil in 1915, the people of Coffee County, Alabama, changed their outlook on farming, switched to planting peanuts, and found prosperity. Third, we can choose to keep on trusting God. When ordered by King Nebuchadnezzar of Babylon to worship a gold statue or face death, three Hebrew youths replied their God would deliver them. "But even if he doesn't," they said, "we will not worship your god." (Daniel 3:18) As we remember those brave young men who lived over two thousand years ago, we learn that, with faith, even the most frustrating disappointments can become fruitful.

24

Ecumenical

In 1892 Sir Wilfred Grenfell, a British medical missionary, was sent to Labrador, a large peninsula in northeastern Canada. He found the white settlers, the Eskimos, and the Indians there suffering from much illness, especially beriberi and tuberculosis, in an area where there were no doctors. Within three months he treated more than 900 patients. Grenfell spent the next forty years serving the people there. Once he spoke about his work in a New England Congregational church, and told the people how he had to amputate the leg of a Roman Catholic woman in Labrador, but he had no artificial limb for her. After the service, a Methodist woman said she had an artificial limb that had been worn by her Presbyterian husband until he died. Sir Wilfred returned to Labrador with the leg. Later, he explained: "When I, an Episcopalian, took that Presbyterian leg given to me by a Methodist woman in a Congregational church and fitted it on my Roman Catholic friend, it enabled her to walk perfectly!" That's a vivid example of the Ecumenical Movement in action.

The word *ecumenical* comes from the Greek word "oikoumene," referring to the inhabited world and meaning world-embracing. The Ecumenical Movement seeks to promote unity among all Christians. It was first organized at the International Missionary Conference held in Edinburgh in 1910. An Episcopal bishop, Charles Brent, attended the Edinburgh Conference, caught a vision of Christian unity, and worked for the first World Conference on Faith and Order held at Lausanne, Switzerland, in 1927. In 1938, at Utrecht, Holland, plans were made for a World Council of Churches, inaugurated at Amsterdam in 1948. In 1962, Pope John XXIII convened the Second Vatican Council (1962-1965) which encouraged Roman Catholics to participate in the Ecumenical Movement. Jesus knew unity among his people was necessary for the credibility of his mission. He prayed: "May they be one, so that the world may believe that you sent me."

25

Esprit de corps

When Frank first went to college, the campus was unfamiliar to him. The curriculum wasn't what he expected. He attended classes and obeyed the rules, but he didn't feel part of things. After a while, though, he caught on. He felt himself becoming a part of the place. Its traditions and enthusiasms were getting to him. He was no longer just going through school; the school was going through him! He had been caught up in the esprit de corps of the school. The phrase *esprit de corps* is a French phrase which, literally, means spirit of the body. The reference to "the body" is to a group of people engaged in the same activity. The group's sense of pride, unity, common interests, and duties is its esprit de corps.

Seven weeks after Jesus' death and resurrection, his followers, gathered in Jerusalem, experienced an enthusiasm for Jesus which they interpreted as God's holy esprit de corps, blowing through them like a refreshing breeze. God's motivating, enlightening Presence they called his "Spirit" (from the old words meaning "wind" or "breath"). When Christians looked back at what happened at Bethlehem, they remembered how God assumed human nature in the womb of Mary as she was overshadowed by the Spirit. Likewise, when Christians looked back at what happened in Jerusalem at Pentecost, they saw how God took a new body, a social body, from humanity, by the power of the Holy Spirit. That new social body is, in Paul's words, the church, the body of Christ. With its Head (Christ) in heaven, this Spirit-filled body is God's living, visible instrument for his work in the world. Individual converts didn't combine to form the church. It was there before them. Conversion to Christ leads, necessarily, to incorporation in his social body, where we experience God's holy esprit de corps. (1 Corinthians 12:12-27)

26

Esteem

"Born to lose" were the words tattooed on the back of the young man's hand. Dr. Norman Vincent Peale pondered how that slogan must have also been tattooed on the mind of the young man who helped him down the steps from the stage in a large auditorium where Dr. Peale had spoken. At the bottom of the steps stood a pretty young woman who said, "Dr. Peale, I'm a nobody, but I just wanted to meet you." Those two persons are typical of many who are plagued by feelings of low self-esteem. The word *esteem* comes from the Latin word "aestimare" which means to value. Your self-esteem indicates your feelings of personal worth. Nothing is more decisive for your life than your level of self-esteem. Persons with low self-esteem tend to be self-haters who are convinced of their inferiority, feel unlovable, and see God as unloving, rejecting, and vindictive. Even those with average self-esteem are self-doubters who question their value, feel they must earn the love of others, and believe in a God whose love they must merit by unending achievements. Significantly, a recent Gallup poll indicates only one out of three Americans have a strong self-esteem.

"Don't underrate yourself," says the Book of Ecclesiasticus in the Apocrypha. "A low opinion of yourself leads to sin." (Ecclesiasticus 4:20) Sin as an act of thought or word or deed is preceded by sin as a fact, a condition in human nature, characterized by a sense of inadequacy, insecurity, and anxiety. I believe this is the core of the human detachment and distrust we call "original sin." Fearful, insecure people overreact by the traditional sins of pride, anger, lust, discouragement, envy, greed, and gluttony. An old Edinburgh weaver used to pray, "O God, help me to hold a high opinion of myself." Jesus answered that universal cry for personal worth by teaching us to call God "our Father" and by showing us the ultimate worth of persons. "We love because he first loved us," wrote St. John. That's how we learn to love ourselves.

27

Excess Baggage

In the last century, a tourist from America paid a visit to a famous Polish rabbi named Hofetz Chaim. The tourist was amazed to see the rabbi lived in one simple room filled with books, plus a table and a bench. "Rabbi," asked the tourist, "where is your furniture?" Rabbi Hofetz Chaim replied, "Where is yours?" "Mine?" asked the puzzled American. "But I'm only a visitor here. I'm only passing through." The rabbi looked at him, smiled, and said, "You're only a visitor? You're only passing through? So am I." Compared to the age of this old world, we're only "passing through," too! Therefore, now is a good time for us to check our lives for *excess baggage* and learn to travel lightly.

While Jesus was on his final journey to Jerusalem, to confront his nation with his claim, he stopped to see two sisters, Mary and Martha, who lived in a small village called Bethany, two miles from Jerusalem. Mary sat down and listened to Jesus' conversation, but her sister, Martha, drove herself to distraction preparing an elaborate meal. Hot and bothered, Martha said to Jesus, "Don't you care that my sister is leaving me to do the serving all by myself? Tell her to help me!" But Jesus answered, "Martha, Martha, you worry and fret about so many things. And yet few are needed, indeed only one." Are you complicating your life with "excess baggage" in the form of things you own or want to own, in the attachments you've formed, in the negative attitudes that weigh down your heart? Sailors say after a boat has been in the water for six months, it can pick up two or three inches of barnacles. That layer of barnacles can weigh 100 tons on an ocean liner, and can reduce the liner's speed by more than ten percent. Regularly the boat has to have the "excess baggage" scraped off. Examine your life, identify and drop your "excess baggage," and learn to travel lightly!

28

Expectations

A farmer was walking through his fields one day when he tripped over a one-gallon glass jug in his pumpkin patch. He eyed the jug for a moment, then decided to try an experiment. He poked a small pumpkin through the neck of the jug, being careful not to break the vine, and left it there. When the time for the pumpkin harvest came, the farmer again found the glass jug. The pumpkin had filled it completely. However, when it reached the limits of the container, it had stopped growing. The farmer broke the jug and had a pumpkin that had taken the jug's exact size and shape.

Into what kinds of mental containers do you put your *expectations?* This word comes from two Latin words: "Ex" (out of) and "spectare" (to look). Our expectations are the glasses through which we look out at the world. When two blind men asked Jesus to restore their sight, he said: "Let your prayer be answered in proportion to your faith." (Matthew 9:29) We could paraphrase Jesus' words: "According to your expectations, be it done to you."

First, you can have great expectations of yourself. Oliver Wendell Holmes said sadly: "Most folks die with all their music still in them." Psychologist William James commented: "The average person does not utilize one-tenth of his potentialities." Second, you can have great expectations of others. Jesus knew how important it is to expect the best from people, because people will either live down to what we suspect of them or they will live up to what we expect of them. Third, you can have great expectations of God. William Carey, the eighteenth century Oriental scholar and English missionary to India, used to say: "Expect great things from God; attempt great things for God!" You can have the romance of such great expectations when you realize what high hopes God has for you!

29

Failure

Mrs. Helen Ireland of Auburn, California, probably holds the record for being the quickest to fail a driver's test. She failed it in about the first second. She got into the car, said "Good morning," to the examiner and started the engine. She mistook the accelerator for the clutch and shot straight through the wall of the Department of Motor Vehicles. The examiner was led home in a state of shock, still clutching his clipboard. It was Mrs. Ireland's ninth time to fail the test.

The word *failure* comes from the Latin verb "fallere," to deceive, to disappoint. When you fail, you feel life has deceived and cheated you. One man who failed wrote: "Life is a jest and all things show it; I thought so once, but now I know it!" People who have not succeeded in being or doing what they wanted are prone to say, "What's the use?"

Charles Kettering, a former inventor and research consultant for General Motors, said: "The job of the educator is to teach people how to fail intelligently." Jesus of Nazareth is the great educator who teaches us invaluable lessons through our failures. Jesus can use our failures to show us our partnership with humanity and himself. Jesus himself experienced failure in his attempt to convert the nation and to transform the apostle Judas. Jesus can use our failures to give us a new perspective. Frank Woolworth's first effort to start a five-cent store in Utica, New York, was a dismal failure. That experience gave him a new insight and made him move to Lancaster, Pennsylvania, where he found success among the thrifty Pennsylvania Dutch. Finally, Jesus can use our failures to open our eyes to the possibility of rising above defeat. An old book about using unpromising materials around the house was called "Adventures with Discarded Materials." That sums up well what Jesus did with people who had failed. He showed them they could rise again!

30

Fear

"As night goes round the earth there are hundreds of thousands who should be sleeping, lying awake fearing a bully, fearing a cruel competitor, fearing lest they cannot make good, fearing some illness they cannot comprehend," wrote H. G. Wells. The word *fear* comes from the German word "(ge) fahr," which means danger, peril, and, basically, a trap. When you feel fearful, you have anxiety and agitation caused by the presence or nearness of some danger, evil, or pain. I believe our basic fears are caused by the "Dreadful D's": disappointment, disparagement, distress, disease, debilitation, destitution, dependency, death, and damnation. We need a way to handle our fears. High, positive, practical religion can do that for us.

The first thing we can do with our fears is to face them. In *Moby Dick,* the captain said, "I will have no man on my boat who does not fear a whale." Fear of some things is indeed the beginning of wisdom! We try to give our children some healthy fears about playing with matches, about bottles labeled "Poison," and, a little later, about the dangers of drugs and herpes.

The second thing we can do with our fears is to grace them. Grace is a gift of God. You can grace your fears by looking on them as gifts from God. Fear of disease, for example, has been a stimulus to medical research. Fear of ignorance has been a spur to education. "Education," said Angelo Patri, "consists in being afraid at the right time."

The third thing we can do with our fears is to place them. Playwright George Bernard Shaw was painfully shy. Yet he overcame his fear of public speaking because he was so intent on delivering the message he had. He did not solve his fears; he dissolved them by placing them into the fiery enthusiasm of a mighty purpose.

31

Gamble

At a funeral of an Atlantic City gambler, the pastor asserted, "Spike is not dead; he only sleeps." From Spike's gambling friends in the congregation came a voice that said, "I've got $100 that says he's dead!" Some people say Lady Godiva was the world's greatest gambler because she put everything she had on a horse. Ponder these two evaluations of gambling. Newspaper columnist, Heywood Broun, wrote: "The urge to gamble is so universal and its practice so pleasurable that I assume it must be evil." However, a Christian pastor, J. Wallace Hamilton, found a deeper significance in gambling. Over thirty years ago, Hamilton, the pastor of a drive-in, walk-in church in Pasadena, Florida, wrote: "Gambling . . . is the degrading, sinful misuse of the noble instinct of adventure, of that God-given capacity for high enterprise."

The word *gamble* comes from the Old English word "gamenian," meaning to enjoy playing, to experience the exhilaration of taking a daring risk. On Good Friday, we recall, the gamblers gathered at the cross on Calvary. First, there were the gamblers beneath the cross. Four Roman soldiers divided Jesus' clothes and gambled for his robe. (John 19:24) Second, there was the gambler on the cross. G. Studdert Kennedy, an Anglican priest, wrote: "He was a gambler, too, my Christ; He took His life and threw it for a world redeemed." Jesus bet his life that the plan of God will eventually prevail and the highest possibilities in man can be redeemed and realized. Third, there was the Gambler above the cross. God the Father took the daring risk of creating persons with whom he shared the gifts of creative imagination and freedom of choice. Those divine gifts establish human beings as persons who can respond, rather than puppets whom God can manipulate to do, inevitably, his bidding.

32

God's Quality

Aurelius Augustinus was converted to Christianity in A.D. 386 by the writings and sermons of Ambrose, the bishop of Milan. Ten years later Aurelius became a bishop himself and served at Hippo on the coast of northern Africa, in the area we now call Algeria. It is said, one day Augustine (as he is called today) was walking along the seashore pondering how God could be One and yet Three. Suddenly he stopped and watched a child who was carrying a cup of ocean water to a small hole he had dug in the sand. "What are you doing?" asked Augustine. The child replied, "I'm trying to pour the ocean into this hole." The bishop laughed and said, "That's impossible." The child stared into his eyes and said, "It is no more impossible than for you to put Almighty God into your small mind."

If we take that story to mean, figuratively speaking, God is so immense the sheer quantity of God makes him incomprehensible, then that is surely true. Yet even a cupful of the Atlantic Ocean is enough to be taken into a laboratory and from it to learn the quality of the whole ocean. This is how our forefathers in the faith were able to speak of God. They dipped into the immeasurable ocean of Divinity and lifted up small measures captured in pictures, words, symbols, images drawn from human experience. In the Bible, therefore, *God's quality* is symbolized by such images as: rock, fortress, father, mother, husband, friend, shepherd. If every man is made in the image of God, then the better the man, the better the image of God. In Jesus, I see the perfect Man, a vessel full of God. While I may be unable to see the sheer quantity of God in him, yet I can see the quality and nature of Divine Love in that transparent human life. That's why Jesus said, "Anyone who has seen me has seen the Father." (John 14:9)

33

Good

"In the beginning of time God created everything, step by step. Slowly, wonderfully, he shaped form out of chaos, gently molding with his mighty hands day and night, lands and seas, grass and fruit trees, the sun, the moon, the stars, birds, fish, cattle, and finally, a man and a woman. Day after day he smiled approvingly at the result of each day's labor. 'Good,' he said, 'it's all good, very good'." This is how Walter Albritton has paraphrased the creation story in Genesis, which ends with these words: "And God saw all that he had made, and it was very good." (Genesis 1:31)

What does the word good mean in that text? Obviously, it does not mean simply what profits human beings, since the word good is used several times in the narrative before man is created. Rather, something is *good* when it fulfills the purpose for which it was made. A good typewriter, for example, is one that does the job for which it was designed.

Why does the divine "Yes" of God's approval ring out as he surveys the goodness of his creation? First, God calls nature good because it is what he designed it to be: the impartial, dependable, uniform stage on which the moral drama of man's history can be enacted. As Shakespeare said, "All the world's a stage, and all the men and women merely players." Second, God calls man good because he is what God intended him to be, namely "the image of God." Man is the mirror-image of God because, in his power of choice, he reflects the Creator's freedom. While man has misused this gift of freedom, it is still an essential part of his nature. This is the original goodness of man which precedes "original sin." You can't have a bad egg on your hands unless it was first a good egg. While the sins of men have broken the heart of God (the inner meaning of the cross of Christ), he still respects our freedom, but says with divine care, "I will never give up on you!" "He goes looking for the one that got lost until he finds it." (Luke 15:4)

34

Goodness and Mercy

"I fled Him, down the nights and down the days; I fled Him, down the arches of the years." Those words begin Francis Thompson's poem, "The Hound of Heaven." Thompson sketches the drama of God pursuing a soul. In that poem Francis Thompson may have been telling his own story. Born in 1859, at Lancashire in northern England, he intended to be a priest, but his physician-father urged him to study medicine. Unable to pass his exams, he went to London, in 1885, where he lived as a tramp and a drug addict. He earned a little money fetching cabs and selling matches. In 1887, he sent some poems he wrote to Wilfred and Alice Meynell, editors of a magazine. They befriended him and helped him to overcome his addiction to opium. In his most godless moments, Thompson still felt hounded and hunted down by God. He wrote his great poem "The Hound of Heaven," after meditating on these words from Psalm 23: "Surely goodness and mercy shall follow me all the days of my life."

In ancient Israel, a shepherd went ahead of his sheep and his dogs brought up the rear. The dogs' main business was to keep the sheep together. If a sheep fell behind, tempted by some attractive wayside plant, the dogs who followed the flock hounded the sheep back where he belonged. With marvelous insight, old King David, the author of Psalm 23, portrayed God's *goodness and mercy* as the dogs that hunt us down and hound us back to the true paths. In recent times, Dr. Abraham Maslow, a psychologist, has likewise recognized this need for stimulus and challenge to move a person to develop his God-given potential. Goodness and mercy hunts us out of our laziness, our trifling, our search for selfish pleasures. God will not give up on us! God's hounds bark behind us and, as Francis Thompson wrote in the final words of his poem, God himself beckons before us: "Rise, clasp My hand and come!"

35

Growing Pains

Growing pains is a term that refers to pains in the limbs or joints during childhood and youth. The term is used in a figurative sense about troubles that occur when something new is just developing. In the experience of Jesus, we can see reflected some of our own "growing pains."

First, there are growing pains in relation to the family. When the boy Jesus was twelve years old, he accompanied his parents to the Temple in Jerusalem. On the way back to Nazareth, Mary and Joseph thought Jesus was with his friends among the other travelers. When they couldn't find him that evening, they went back to Jerusalem to search for him there. Three days later, they discovered him sitting with the teachers of Law in the Temple. From that time there were "growing pains" as Jesus moved beyond his family's understanding of him. (John 7:5)

Second, there are growing pains in relation to forefathers. In "The Sermon on the Mount," Jesus says repeatedly, "You have learned that our forefathers were told . . . But what I tell you is this." (Matthew 5:21, 27, 31, 33, 38, 43) Jesus suffered growing pains as he went beyond the faith of his fathers.

Third, there are growing pains in relation to friends. At the peak of his popularity, Jesus "began to speak plainly to his disciples about going to Jerusalem and what would happen to him there." (Matthew 16:21) When he spoke about suffering, rejection, and crucifixion, his friend "Peter took him aside and chided him. 'You shouldn't say things like that,' he told Jesus." (Mark 8:32) Jesus suffered growing pains as he went beyond the advice of his friends.

Because Jesus shared these growing pains with us, the New Testament says: "Son though he was, he learned obedience in the school of suffering." (Hebrews 5:8).

36

Grudge

Anemia was the girl's problem. After several months of unsuccessful treatment, her physician decided to send her to the medical officer in the district where she worked. He wanted to get his permission to send her to a mountain sanatorium. The patient returned to her physician one week later with the permit from the medical officer. On the permit was this notation: "On analyzing the blood, however, I do not arrive at anything like the figures you quote." The physician checked his original figures, drew a fresh sample of blood from the girl, and rushed to his laboratory to find the blood count really had changed. He returned to his office and asked the girl, "Has anything out of the ordinary happened in your life since your last visit?" The girl replied, "Yes, something has happened. I have suddenly been able to forgive someone against whom I bore a nasty grudge; and all at once I felt I could at last say, 'Yes', to life." That story about the high cost of holding a grudge was reported by Dr. Paul Tournier in his book, "A Doctor's Casebook in the Light of the Bible."

"If a man harbours a grudge against another, is he to expect healing from the Lord?" asked a Jewish teacher named Jesus, the son of Sirach, who wrote those words about 180 B.C. in a book called "Ecclesiasticus" (29:3) found in the Apocrypha. The word *grudge* means ill-will, a sullen feeling against another, an anger or dislike of long standing. It comes from the Old French word "groucher," meaning to murmur or grumble. One woman who certainly understands that feeling is Julie Nixon Eisenhower, who said this in 1974: "Although only 26, two years ago I felt mentally middle-aged. I found that holding grudges and allowing bitterness to fester mutilated my spirit." Julie reflected on these words from Paul's Letter to the Church in Colossae: "Be gentle and ready forgive; never hold grudges. Remember, the Lord forgave you, so you must forgive others." (Colossians 3:13, LB) From the standpoint of health, the moral is clear: bury your grudges or your grudges will bury you!

37

Hard-Boiled

In the early days of the American frontier, women used lye soap and often washed their family's clothes in an open stream. These clothes tended to become gray very quickly. Once a month, therefore, the wise housewife would boil her load of wash in a black iron pot. Then she starched the best pieces with a paste, made in her own kitchen. Sometimes she would get her husband's Sunday shirts too stiff. He would then accuse his wife of boiling the clothes so long that they became hard. The phrase *hard-boiled* has passed into our language as an adjective, used figuratively, to refer to persons. We might talk about "a hard-boiled veteran of two wars." We use the phrase to mean someone not easily moved by feelings. Popular wisdom says, "Happy are the hard-boiled."

In contrast to the hard-boiled, Jesus said, "Blessed are those who mourn, for they shall be comforted." To mourn is to be sensitive enough to feel sorrow. In J. B. Phillips' translation of the New Testament, he renders this text as follows: "How happy are those who know what sorrow means, for they will be given courage and comfort." As a biologist ranks living creatures, in the scale of life, according to their sensitivity to pain, so Jesus grades human beings by their ability to mourn. First, there is happiness in being sensitive to our own sorrows. There is a blessed relief in being able to express our grief that is denied to those who steel their hearts. "Jesus wept." Second, we know the deep happiness of being fully human when we are sensitive to other people's sorrows. Part of the cost of following Jesus is being sensitive to the pain around us. Third, the happiness of divine forgiveness comes to those who are sensitive to God's sorrows. The cross of Jesus brings us to repentance as it reminds us vividly what our sins do to the God who loves us.

38

Healthy Religion

"It is worth-while to look at the types of character that Jesus admires. How many of the parables turn on energy. Thus, for instance, the parable of the talents turns on energetic thinking and decisive action; and these are the things that Jesus admires." So wrote T. R. Glover in his book, "The Jesus of History." Think of the energetic people whom Jesus made the heroes of his parables: the crooked judge (Luke 18:2); the enterprising pearl merchant (Matthew 13:45); the dishonest accountant (Luke 16:8); the wasteful young man (Luke 15:13). No less energetic and decisive are the tenant farmers in another of Jesus' shocking parables. Those farmers will stop at nothing, even murder, to get their hands on the estate where they worked (Matthew 21:33-43).

If Jesus rated energy so highly, that gives us a clue to the kind of religion he considered healthy and positive. From research and reflection, I believe there are five qualities in a healthy religious approach to life. First, healthy religion is energetic. Look back at the characters Jesus cited and you can see that. Second, healthy religion is elevating, not depressing. Think how often the word "joy" and "good cheer" were on Jesus' lips! Healthy religion, like a refreshing breeze, comes with the unexpected gift of an unexpected lift. Third, healthy religion in enlarging, not belittling. Of course, religious people can major in minors, but, at its best, religion continually enlarges our view of God, of goodness, and of the greatness and potential in human lives. Fourth, healthy religion is empowering, not enfeebling. Granted, some people and churches use religion as a spiritual narcotic; nevertheless, at its best, religion gives inner reinforcement for the quest of freedom, fairness, and fulfillment. Fifth, healthy religion is ego-freeing and God-centered. Instead of identifying God's will with our own desires, Jesus taught us to pray, "Yet not what I want, but what You want." (Mark 14:36)

39

Hero

Robert Redford's movie about baseball, "The Natural," confirms the words of educator Jacques Barzun: "Whoever wants to know about the heart and mind of America had better learn baseball." Redford portrays Roy Hobbs, the farm boy whose dream is to become the best baseball player ever in the major leagues. On the night of his father's death, in 1918 on the Hobbs' farm, lightning struck a giant oak tree, splitting it in two. Roy fashioned a baseball bat out of a piece of wood and named it "Wonderboy." In the movie, Roy is a hero whose life is traced to the final, decisive game. In Bernard Malamud's 1952 novel on which the movie is based, one character explains: "Without heroes, we're all plain people and don't know how far we can go . . . it's their function to be the best." The movie raises for us the question: "How do you define a hero?"

The word *hero* comes from the Greek word "heros," which in turn seems to be derived from an Indo-European base "ser," to watch over and protect. In ancient mythology and legend, a hero was a man of great strength and courage, favored by the gods and, in part, descended from them. The word hero has come to stand for any man admired for his courage, nobility, or exploits. Such a person is regarded as an ideal or model. Consider what varied personalities have been heroes to some in our century: Churchill and Hitler, Edward R. Murrow and Joseph McCarthy, Martin Luther King, Jr. and George Wallace, Norman Lear and Jerry Falwell. "Stars" of television, motion pictures, rock music, and politics serve as heroes who influence people's aspirations and behavior. Because these heroes serve as role models, they capture our imagination. This baseball allegory, "The Natural," brings us face to face with a soul-searching truth: Tell me who your heroes are, and I will tell you what your values are!

40

Heroes

Researchers for the *World Almanac and Book of Facts* asked 2,000 American eighth-grade students to name prominent people they admired and wanted to be like. Most frequently mentioned, by the students as their *heroes,* were celebrities such as Burt Reynolds, Richard Pryor, Steve Martin and the late John Belushi. Who are your heroes? Who is your self-ideal? I believe those whom we choose as heroes are those who have wrestled with problems and coped with them in striking ways. A hero affects us in four ways. First, a hero captures our attention. In the Bible is a list of the heroes among King David's warriors. One of those heroes was a man named Benaiah "who went down into a pit and killed a lion on a snowy day." (2 Samuel 23:20) Because we face problems that stalk us like lions, we admire Benaiah, whose action captures our attention.

Second, a hero crystalizes our intention. The lion Benaiah faced strayed up from the area near the Jordan River and was stranded in a snowstorm. The presence of that lion was not under Benaiah's control. However, what Benaiah could control was his reaction to the problems he faced. That kind of self-control is a purpose worth having. Benaiah's example helps us to crystalize just such an intention.

Third, a hero cultivates our retention. Although it was a snowy day and the lion was in a pit, Benaiah did not run away; he held his ground before the lion. Benaiah's courage, in the face of unfavorable circumstances, encourages our retention, our holding on when the going gets tough. As a Norwegian proverb says: "A hero is one who knows how to hold on one minute longer."

Fourth, a hero catalyzes our extension. Just as a certain substance can spark a chemical reaction, so a heroic figure causes us to enlarge our outlook and to expand our efforts toward our goals.

41

Holy Week

Holy Week is the last week of Lent, beginning with Palm Sunday and ending on Easter Saturday. During Holy Week, the events of Jesus' last days of earthly life are commemorated. On Palm Sunday, Jesus dramatized his claim to be Israel's Messiah by riding into his nation's capital, Jerusalem. There he drove dishonest merchants from the Temple. On Monday, Jesus cursed a fig tree, one of the national symbols for Israel, as an acted parable of judgment on the nation's fruitlessness. On Tuesday, Jesus taught people in the Temple, using his customary riddle-like stories called parables. During this time, he confronted the leaders of Israel's religious life. On Wednesday, Jesus' enemies planned their conspiracy against him and made a deal with Judas, one of the twelve apostles, to betray him.

On Thursday, Jesus sent his friends to make preparations for the Passover meal in an upstairs room in Jerusalem. That evening, while eating with his friends, Jesus identified himself with bread and wine as signs of his sacrifice. After the meal, he went to a private garden named "Gethsemane" where he was later arrested. The arrest was made secretly because Jesus was a popular hero with the majority of the Jewish people. (Matthew 26:3-5; Luke 22:2) During the night, Jesus faced two trials: a religious trial before the high priest, Caiaphas, and a political trial before the Roman governor, Pontius Pilate. On Friday, Jesus was nailed to a cross by Roman soldiers at nine o'clock in the morning. (Mark 15:25) His dead body was taken down and buried before sunset. On Saturday, Jesus, separated from his body, went to the place of departed spirits (Paradise) to announce the Good News to those who were awaiting the general resurrection. (1 Peter 3:19; 4:6) On Sunday, Jesus' spirit returned to his body, transformed it, and then, passing through his grave clothes and from the sealed tomb, was raised to newness of life by the power of God.

42

Hope

"Where there is no faith in the future, there is no power in the present." Those words come from a man who lived in the town of Flagstaff, Maine, years ago. The town was to be taken over as part of a hydroelectric development. Because a dam was being built, Flagstaff would soon be under water. In the months before this was accomplished, all improvements and repairs to homes and other buildings came to a dead stop. People in the town said to themselves: "What's the sense of painting the house if it's going to be covered with water in six months? Why fix anything?" Week by week the little town became more and more bedraggled, forlorn, and shabby. It went to seed, long before the waters came, because it lost *hope.*

"In all things it is better to hope than despair," wrote Goethe. Tennyson spoke of "the mighty hopes that make us men." The Apostle Paul, in his Letter to Christians in Rome, said: "We are saved by hope." (Romans 8:24) As we are about to enter tomorrow, how can we put hope into our brains instead of putting dope (alcohol and chemicals) into our veins? First, recognize your undeveloped possibilities. You can be more than you are now. You can do more than you have done so far. A famous psychiatrist once said: "There are vast undamaged areas in every human life. These undamaged areas must be discovered, then used as the base for a new beginning." Secondly, rely on the God of Abraham, Isaac, and Jacob, the God and Father of Jesus. The psalmist affirmed: "I depend on God alone; I put my hope in him." (Psalm 62:5) This kind of positive, personal faith will give you stronger morale in the face of discouragements. It will put deeper meaning into your life. It will give you the motivation to grow toward the whole, complete person God designed you to be. The God of hope can fill you with enough inspiration that you will be able to make those positive resolutions that lead to personal revolutions!

43

Idolatry

After Moses and the people of Israel escaped from Egypt, they wandered for many years in the Sinai peninsula. At one time, a plague of poisonous serpents attacked the people. Many died of snakebite. Moses received a divine inspiration to make a bronze serpent and put it on the top of a pole. Anyone who had been bitten could look at that bronze serpent and be healed. (Numbers 21:8-9) The bronze serpent, from the days of Moses, became a national relic of the Hebrew nation. Gradually, it became the object of superstitious worship. Six hundred years after the days of Moses, a king named Hezekiah ruled the southern kingdom of Judah. The record of his reign states: "He destroyed the pagan places of worship, broke the stone pillars, and cut down the image of the goddess Asherah. He also broke in pieces the bronze snake that Moses had made." (2 Kings 18:4)

In that ancient story is an example of the origins of *idolatry.* The bronze serpent which Moses made was meant to be a reminder of God. In ancient mythology, the serpent was a symbol for wisdom and healing. In Greece, the god of healing, Aesculapuis, had a rod entwined by a serpent as his magical instrument of healing. In Israel, that bronze replica of a serpent was intended to be a reminder that healing comes from God. Centuries later, the Jewish author of "The Wisdom of Solomon" wrote this: "You gave them a healing symbol, the bronze snake, to remind them of what your Law requires." (Wisdom 16:7) In the course of time, the symbol, which was intended to be a reminder of God, was treated by the people as itself a god! Whenever we turn an aid to worship into an object of worship, idolatry rises again. Written forms of worship, arrangements of church government, venerable religious language, and historic church buildings can all be treated in a way that turns them into modern idols.

44

Inadequate

Two cows were grazing alongside I-95 in Bucks County when a tank truck of milk, on its way to the distributor, happened to pass by. On the side of the truck in big red letters was a sign which read: "This milk is pasteurized, homogenized, standardized, and has Vitamin A added." One cow turned to the other and remarked, "That makes you feel sort of inadequate, doesn't it?"

If you're facing some trouble right now and saying, "I can't stand it," or you're facing your work and saying, "I can't do it," then you know this feeling of inadequacy. The word *inadequate* comes from three Latin words: "in" (not); "ad" (to); and "aequus" (equal). When you feel inadequate, you feel you're not equal to the problems you face or the work you have to do. Low, negative religion puts people down and increases the sense of inadequacy. High, positive religion helps people to feel adequate to meet life by reminding them of God's secret strategy: "God chose what the world looks down on and despises and thinks is nothing, in order to destroy what the world thinks is important." (1 Corinthians 1:28)

God does four things to make us feel adequate to face life. He embraces us, welcoming us when we feel most unworthy. God encourages us when we feel most incompetent by reminding us of his unlikely instruments: Moses felt inadequate because he stuttered; Gideon felt unqualified because he was poor and insignificant; Jeremiah felt unfit because he was young; Peter felt unworthy because he had failed. God employs us because he loves to accomplish mighty things by humble means. Great consequences can flow from small causes. Finally, God empowers us by awakening us to the possibilities he has put into us. All great living begins with sense of the possible. Jesus showed us the way when he said: "Everything is possible for the person who has faith." (Mark 9:23)

45

Interruption

Jack lived on an island in the middle of a river. An unusual amount of rain threatened to swell the river and flood Jack's island. The mayor of the town, on shore, sent a man in a canoe to the island. The man shouted, "Jack, there's a flood coming! Get into the canoe!" Restlessly pacing on the beach, Jack shouted back, "Go away, you're interrupting my concentration! Jesus will save me." The mayor sent a second man in a motorboat with the same warning, but Jack repeated, "Go away, you're interrupting my concentration! Jesus will save me." Finally the mayor himself flew to the island in a helicopter and pleaded with Jack to get in. Restlessly pacing back and forth on the roof of his house, Jack shouted back, "Go away, you're interrupting my concentration! Jesus will save me." Suddenly a wall of water swept Jack from the roof and he woke up in Paradise on the other side of death. "Lord," Jack said, "I'm disappointed that you didn't come and save me." Jesus smiled, patted him on the back, and said, "Jack, I sent a canoe, a motorboat, and a helicopter to save you, but you called them interruptions!"

Earthly interruptions may well be heavenly eruptions as God bursts out of eternity into time. The word *interruption* comes from two Latin words "inter" (between) and "rumpere" (to break). An interruption breaks in upon our thinking, or talking, or working and makes us pause. The Lord, like a good shepherd, interrupts his sheep's restlessness, makes them lie down in green pastures they don't even recognize, and leads them to concealed, tranquil waters. (Psalm 23:2) When loving parents brought little children to Jesus, his disciples looked on it as an interruption, and scolded them. Jesus, however, used that earthly interruption for a heavenly eruption, an occasion for a new insight to break in on the disciples' stale thinking. The next time you experience an interruption, ask yourself, "What is God trying to tell me?"

46

Jesus

"The consciousness of the presence of God has come to millions of men and women through Jesus," wrote Solomon B. Freehof, a distinguished Jewish preacher. "He is still the living comrade of countless lives. No Moslem ever sings, 'Mohammed, lover of my soul,' nor does any Jew say of Moses, 'I need thee every hour.' He brought God near to men through his presence. He made the Divine personal for myriads of worshippers."

Why do people believe so intensely in *Jesus* Christ? I would offer you four reasons. First, people believe in Jesus because of his character. He has the marvelous knack of seeing extraordinary possibilities in ordinary people. That positive, liberating character haunts us and heals us of our self-despisings. Second, people believe in Jesus because of his claims. During his trial before Caiaphas, the high priest, and the Jewish Council, Caiaphas asked Jesus directly: "Are you the Messiah, the Son of the Blessed God?" Jesus' answer made his claim direct and explicit: "I am." (Mark 14:61-62) That claim forces us to make a choice: deceived? deceiving? divine? Third, people believe in Jesus because of his commitment. Though he recognized that the cross lay ahead, he remained loyal to the royal within himself. "I was born," Jesus said, "and came into the world for this one purpose, to speak about the truth." (John 18:37) Fourth, people believe in Jesus because of his conquests. He conquered death and liberated us from fear of the grave. He conquered time by striking history with such an impact that we date our years from his coming. He conquered space by assuming a new, social body, his church, through which he continues his work of teaching, guiding and making lives whole. No wonder Episcopal Biship Phillips Brooks saluted him by saying: "Jesus Christ, the condescension of divinity, and the exaltation of humanity!"

47

Jesus' Name

The miracle and mystery of Christmas is summed up in the name of that baby born in Bethlehem so long ago. Joseph, his foster-father, was instructed by the angel: "You will name him Jesus — because he will save his people from their sins." (Matthew 1:21)

Each letter of that name teaches us a lesson. The "J" reminds us Jesus is Jewish. He is a true son of Israel, raised in the traditions of his fathers in the faith. The God of Jesus is the God of Abraham, Isaac, and Jacob. Jesus said: "It is from the Jews that salvation comes." (John 4:22) The "E" stands for Emmanuel, the title applied to him means "God is with us." In ancient days, the God of Israel tabernacled among his people in the Tent in the wilderness and made his Presence known to them in the great Temple at Jerusalem. At Bethlehem, God chose to dwell among men in the human nature of Jesus. The "S" stands for Savior. That word goes back to the Greek word "soter," the first century term for a doctor who delivered a person from disease and restored them to wholeness. Jesus thought of himself in this sense. When he was criticized for associating with persons with whom no respectable Jew would have anything to do, Jesus replied: "People who are well do not need a doctor, but only those who are sick." (Mark 2:17) The "U" stands for Jesus' Universal mission and appeal. He chose the star as the last symbol for himself. (Revelation 22:16) A star does not belong exclusively to one nation, but it can be seen by people everywhere. The second "S" stands for Sacrifice. A sacrifice is an expensive gift of love given by someone who cares. In the text summing up the Good News of the Christian message, Jesus said: "God loved the world so much that he gave his only Son" so, as you trust yourself to him, you may not go to pieces, but have life with eternal depth and meaning.

48

Jesus' Popularity

Palm Sunday is the Sunday before Easter. It is the first day of Holy Week. The services of Palm Sunday honor Jesus' triumphant entry into Jerusalem. According to John's account, "They took branches of palm trees and went out to meet him." (John 12:13) Nearly three million persons thronged the city, in those days before the Passover festival of freedom. *Jesus' popularity* with the crowds is clear. "Then the Pharisees said to one another, 'You see, there is nothing you can do; look, the whole world is running after him'." (John 12:19 JB)

Why did the crowds love Christ? First, the crowds loved him for his courage. When Jesus came into Jerusalem on the first Palm Sunday, he was, in the eyes of the authorities, a criminal marked for arrest. (See John 11:57) Despite that fact, Jesus deliberately made a public entrance dramatizing his claim to be king. Second, the crowds loved Christ for his common touch. They saw him as one of themselves, a Jew of the common people. He spoke their familiar dialect, drew his images from their familiar experiences, and even dressed as they did, with tassels on the corners of his garment to show he was a Jew. (See Numbers 15:38-40) Mark testifies: "And the common people heard him gladly." (Mark 12:37) Third, the crowds loved Christ for his caring. When a thoughtful young man approached him with deep questions, the Bible says, "Jesus looked straight at him with love." (Mark 10:21) That could be said of everyone Jesus saw — even Judas, whom he called "Friend" at the very moment of his betrayal. (Matthew 26:50) In a contest for the best definition of a friend, the winning answer was this: "A friend is one who comes in when the rest of the world has gone out." That's how the crowds in Jerusalem felt about Jesus of Nazareth.

49

Jesus' Resurrection

Imagine how early man must have stared in wonder at an egg. It looked like a stone. But, after proper incubation, a chick inside took its beak and started pecking on the shell until it was broken open. Out of the dead thing poked a tiny beak, a head, and the soft warm body of a living bird. A whole new world began for the baby chick. It must have seemed like a miracle to early man — the miracle of new life coming from the world of the dead. That is why the egg has become an Easter symbol, for Christians, of *Jesus' resurrection.*

What difference does Christ's resurrection make for us? First, his resurrection makes a difference in our thinking about death. "If a man die, shall he live again?" asked Job. (14:14) Tombstones in ancient Roman cemeteries said "No," by this inscription: "I was not, I was, I am not, I do not care." Then Easter dawned on the old world and Christ "has broken the power of death and brought life and immortality to light through the Gospel." (2 Timothy 1:10) "Because I live," said Jesus, "you also will live." (John 14:19) Second, Christ's resurrection makes a difference in our thinking about life. How can one be optimistic about life, believe in human possibilities, and have hope, when one sees the cross of Christ as the exhibition of what human stupidity and cruelty can do? Then Easter dawned on the old world and, raising Christ, God gave his assurance to us "what is excellent, as God lives, is permanent." Third, Christ's resurrection makes a difference in our thinking about God. The God of the Greeks lived in undisturbed tranquility, untouched by the cries of his creatures. Then Easter dawned on the old world, revealing a nail-torn Christ, whose scars told us God is not an indifferent spectator of the world's suffering, but an active, sympathetic participant in it.

50

Kingdom of God

When Leslie Weatherhead, the late English pastor, lived in India as a young man, he had a sturdy garden wall around his house. It was a foot thick, built of stone, and cemented over. A tiny seed, probably dropped by a bird, fell into a crack in the cement. When Dr. Weatherhead noticed a little plant growing out of the top of the wall, he cut it off and forgot about it. Dr. Weatherhead went away to serve in the British Army. On his return, he found a healthy little bush had grown on the wall. He removed all he could of it. Later, a monsoon came and, during the storm, the wall collapsed. "Incredible as it may sound," wrote Dr. Weatherhead, "the roots of that plant had gone down and down and displaced stones, broken the cement, and so weakened the whole wall that it fell before the onslaught of rain and wind and tempest."

The incident is an illustration of what Jesus meant by the *Kingdom of God.* Jesus gave the Kingdom the central place in his preaching. However, the word "kingdom" can mislead us. It suggests a territory like the "United Kingdom," or the "Kingdom of Norway." To correct this misunderstanding, some modern translations speak, instead, about the "Reign of God." This helps to make it clear the Kinqdom of God is not a territory, but an activity. It is God exercising his kingship, by his power at work in the world. Like the seed in Dr. Weatherhead's wall, God's power has been at work, raising mankind's attitudes toward children, women, the aged, the weak and ill, the evils of slavery and war. Jesus did not just talk about the Kingdom of God; he is the bearer and the embodiment of it. In his healings, his teachings, and his personality, God's power has broken into history, though we still await its full realization. That's why we pray, "Thy kingdom come." "For Christ must rule until God defeats all enemies and puts them under his feet." (1 Corinthians 15:25)

51

Labor Day

In 1882, a member of the Executive Council of The American Federation of Labor proposed one day in the year be set aside as a general holiday for working people. That man was P. J. McGuire and the day he proposed, the first Monday in September, is called "Labor Day." The Central Labor Union adopted the idea and held a parade and festival on the first Monday in September, 1882. In 1884, the convention of the American Federation of Labor unanimously adopted a resolution that proposed "the first Monday in September each year be set apart as a laborers' national holiday." In a short time, municipal councils and state legislatures were making it a legal holiday. In 1894, Congress passed bills which made *Labor Day* a legal holiday for the entire country.

Labor Day was established to honor all the working people of the nation: those who grow its food, who make its tools and machinery, who build its roads and bridges, who erect its buildings, who sell its goods, and provide services for its people. Though we may sometimes feel the need to "vacate" the place where we work by taking a vacation, I'm sure most of us would agree with Thomas Carlyle who said: "Blessed is the man who has found his work." Another wise man said: "Every man's work is his life preserver." In one of his letters, St. Paul lifted our daily work up into the realm where we see ourselves as fellow workers with the Divine! Paul wrote: "For we are laborers together with God." (1 Corinthians 3:9) This means God has chosen us to be co-creators with him in finishing and perfecting his creation. We join him in the continuing work of healing the human family and building all men into life together in loving community. That's why Jesus said: "My Father has never yet ceased his work, and I am working too." (John 5:17)

52

Letting Go (I)

In the first book of the Divine Library we call "The Bible" (from Greek for "the books") is the story of a man called Lot. Messengers from God came to the city of Sodom, where Lot lived, and told him to take his wife and daughters away from the city. Sodom was about to be destroyed by the judgment of God. As the family fled, the narrative says: "But Lot's wife, behind him, looked back, and she turned into a pillar of salt." (Genesis 19:26) In a literal sense, the woman's body became encrusted with deadly saline particles. In a figurative sense, she refused to let go of the past, became mentally static, spiritually lifeless, and hardened. This human "pillar of salt" has become a striking image of the bitterness of regret. Even Jesus counseled, "Remember Lot's wife." (Luke 17:32) Because she kept on looking back, she failed to master "The Art of Letting Go."

The art of *letting go* involves three actions. First, burn the tree. One day a fruit tree was blown over and uprooted in a farmer's field. A neighbor asked the farmer, "What are you going to do with it?" The farmer replied, wisely, "You see it has fruit on the branches. I'm going to gather the fruit and then burn the tree." Let go your losses, mistakes, regrets, and resentments by "gathering the fruit, and then burning the tree." Second, bathe the wound. Looking back only rubs salt in our emotional wounds. Apply the soothing balm of forgiveness. Don't hold a grudge against yourself! "There is a balm in Gilead to make the wounded whole." Third, bury the dead. More exactly, Jesus said it this way: "Leave the dead to bury their dead . . . No one who sets his hand to the plow and then keeps looking back is fit for the kingdom of God." (Luke 9: 60,62) There are plenty of spiritually dead to arrange funerals! The art of letting go involves the discipline of the forward look.

53

Letting Go (II)

A man was making a trip on the rapids of the Colorado River, where the water rushes quickly over the rocks near the surface. His canoe overturned, but he managed to catch hold of it. He hung on, terrified, with a vice-like grip. Some people saw his desperate situation. One of them crawled out on some rocks, at a bend in the river downstream. As the man came hurtling by, his rescuer caught him by the coat and shouted, "Let go!" The imperiled man was so scared, however, he kept on clutching to the canoe as it swept him downstream to destruction.

There is a time to hold on and a time to let go! The author of the biblical book of Ecclesiastes wrote there is "a time to keep and a time to throw away." (Ecclesiastes 3:6) We need to know the time of *letting go!*

First, possessions need to be let go. Pablo Picasso, the famous artist, once painted murals on the walls of a small apartment as a wedding present to a young couple. These murals were quite valuable. A first and, then, a second child was born. The tiny apartment became cramped and the couple's nerves became frazzled. Reluctantly, they decided to let go of the apartment. In a cottage in the country, they became happier and healthier. Second, practices of the past need to be let go. In Old Testament times, for example, slavery was an accepted practice. But, as James Russell Lowell wrote: "New occasions teach new duties, Time makes ancient good uncouth." Third, persons need to be let go. A mother, for example, really shows her love for her child by letting that child go to realize his possibilities to become an independent human being. "If you love something," an unknown author has written, "set it free. If it comes back to you, it is yours. If it doesn't come back, it never was really yours!"

54

Liberator

In the early days of Israel's history, a divine messenger visited the wife of a man named Manoah. The messenger told her she would conceive and give birth to a son. This boy would grow up to be the *liberator* of his people. He would break the grip of Israel's enemies, the Philistines. Manoah prayed, "Tell us what we are to do with the boy who is to be born." (Judges 13:8) The boy who was born was named Samson. He grew up, lived, loved, warred, and died. Centuries later, the angel of the Lord returned to Israel and told another woman, Mary, she would give birth to another strong man. (Luke 11:22) He, too, would be a liberator of his people, warring against the spiritual "Philistines" of darkness, who enslave and corrupt human life. As we ponder Mary's child, Jesus, the same old question arises: "What are we to do with the boy who is to be born?"

Three attitudes toward Jesus spell three answers to Christmas. First, there is the answer of pugnacity. Herod showed this hostile, belligerent spirit when he "gave orders for the massacre of all children in Bethlehem." (Matthew 2:16) Isn't that violence perpetuated today by a sneer, a stance of superiority, or a sullen silence? Second, there is the answer of preoccupation. The innkeeper of Bethlehem illustrates this answer. He had neither fierce opposition nor furious hatred for Christ, yet his secular priorities induced apathy toward the sacred. Third, there is the answer of perception. When Mary and Joseph took the infant Jesus to the Temple, eight days after his birth, they were met by an old man named Simeon who perceived the significance of Christ and said to Mary: "This child is destined to be a sign which men reject; and you too shall be pierced to the heart." (Luke 2:34-35) The power of perception sees "that God was Man in Palestine, and lives today in Bread and Wine."

55

Life after Death

Life after death is a matter I think about at the beginning of November, because on, November 1, the church celebrates "All Saints' Day," and remembers those who have passed to the next stage of life which Jesus called "Paradise." (Luke 23:43) Yet, I can sympathize with people who dismiss this idea of life after death as wishful thinking. They would probably say: "You don't want to face the fact that your life is going to be snuffed out, so you tell yourself that you'll continue to exist. Be brave enough to face the brutal truth! When a candle is used up or broken, the flame goes out. Likewise, when your body dies, you'll cease to be." This illustration about the candle really shows the opposite of extinction. The light from the used candle continues on through space just as the light from some long exploded star goes on and reaches our eyes.

The survival of our personal individuality was confirmed by Jesus, who said, "If it were not so, I would have told you." (John 14:2) I believe we can affirm four things about that life beyond life. First, it is a vivid conscious life (Luke 9:30; 16:27), not a period of unconscious sleep. Second, it is a life in which one can remember clearly. (Luke 16:25) Third, it is a life when we are gradually shaped and molded to the likeness of Christ. (1 John 3:1-2) Fourth, it is a life of continuing and deepening relationship with Christ. (Philippians 1:23) Surely that last affirmation implies a similar continuation of relationship with those whom we have loved and lost for awhile. This brings us to a startling, comforting conclusion: because of the Lord Jesus and all he has done for human beings, we never see one another for the last time!

56

Limelight

Sir Humphry Davy, a British chemist, isolated calcium oxide in 1808. This substance was popularly known as lime, quicklime, or unslaked lime. Davy demonstrated this lime would produce a brilliant white light when heated to incandescence. Thomas Drummond took advantage of this fact to devise a new type of light for theatrical purposes. In 1816, he placed such a cylinder of lime, heated by a flame, in two different arrangements: behind a lens and in front of a reflector. At first, this new form of illumination was called the "Drummond light," but gradually it became known as *limelight.* In the theatre, it was perfect to highlight the star performer. Although that method of illumination has been surpassed, we still speak of a person who is at the center of public attention as being in the limelight.

During his days in the public eye, Jesus was in the limelight. With startling honesty, the Gospel accounts report four judgments about Christ. First, his enemies said, "He has a demon! He is crazy!" (John 10:20) When you consider Jesus' acts of kindness and healing, you see that only blinding hatred could form such a damning opinion. Second, his friends said, "He is a good man." (John 7:12) Such an opinion seems reasonable, until one reflects on the magnitude of his claims. Third, his Apostle Peter confessed, "You are the Messiah!" (Mark 8:29) That word meant "anointed one," and signified the person chosen by God to deliver his people. Fourth, his doubting Apostle Thomas saw the scars of the risen Christ and said, "My Lord and My God!" (John 20:28) It was after Thomas had learned the importance of doubting his doubts that he saw Jesus truly belonged in the limelight.

57

Lost

"I come here to find myself. It is so easy to get lost in the world." Those words are inscribed on a plaque at the "Singing Tower" at Mountain Lake in central Florida. How do people get lost? When Jesus had to defend his lifestyle toward people who had gotten lost, he told some stories as illustrations. Some people, he said, get lost like sheep who foolishly nibble themselves away from the flock. Other people, Jesus said, get lost like a silver coin, out of circulation and useless in the dust, because or someone's carelessness. Still other people get lost like a young prodigal son, whose wastefulness turned his family inheritance into a personal failure. And some people, Jesus said, get lost like the prodigal son's elder brother, whose selfishness made him jealous, self-righteous, and self-pitying. You can lose your sense of direction by foolishness, wastefulness, selfishness, or the carelessness of others. The word *lost* comes from the word lose, which is derived from the Latin verb "luere," to loose your hold on something, to let it slip away.

Faith's answer to lostness is in the affirmation about God: "He restoreth my soul; he leadeth me in the paths of righteousness for his Name's sake." (Psalm 23:3) Billy Graham once told a story about an American aviator who had to parachute into a jungle in Burma. A Burmese came along, slashing his way through with his machete, trying to get the American aviator out. The American was scared to death, afraid he was going to be captured by the guerrillas. He called out: "Where's the way? Where is the road?" The Burmese, in broken English, turned to him and said: "I'm the way. Follow me!" When you feel lost in the world, remember that's what God is saying to you through Jesus of Nazareth: "I'm the way. Follow me "

58

Luck

Many years ago, begins an old Chinese story, there was a man who had a horse and one son. One day his horse broke out of the corral and fled to the freedom of the hills. "Your horse got out? What bad luck!" said his neighbors. "Why?" the old man asked. "How do you know it's bad luck? Sure enough, the next day the horse came back to his familiar corral for his usual feeding and watering. The horse was leading twelve wild stallions with him. The farmer's son saw the thirteen horses in the corral, slipped out, and locked the gate. Suddenly, the old Chinese man had thirteen horses instead of none. The neighbors heard the news and came chattering to the farmer, "Oh, you've got thirteen horses! What good luck!" The old man answered, "How do you know that it's good luck?" Some days later, his strong young son was trying to break one of the stallions. He was thrown from the horse and broke his leg. The neighbors came back that night and passed another hasty judgment: "Your son broke his leg? What bad luck." The wise father answered them: "How do you know it's bad luck?" Sure enough, a few days later, a Chinese war lord came through the town and conscripted every able-bodied young man, taking them off to war from which they never returned. However, the young son of the famrer was saved from that deadly journey because of his broken leg. Once more the neighbors came to rejoice with the farmer in his good luck and once more the old man said, "How do you know this is good luck?"

The story ends there, although it could go on forever. See the truth in this story: if God alone is ultimate, then God alone is final. If God alone is final, then no event is final, nor can it be properly appraised on the day it happens. No day is good, no day is bad, until all the days are in and life adds them up together. Trust God, therefore, and remember: "There's always tomorrow!"

59

Mansion

In A.D. 627, the monk Paulinus visited King Edwin in northern England, to persuade him to accept Christianity. Picture that old regal hall blazing with torches. A crowd of eager listeners hung intent on the teaching of the Christian missionaries who had just arrived. At last, a grim bearded old earl rose in his place. "Can this new religion," he asked, "tell us what happens after death? The life of man is like a little bird flying through this lighted hall. It enters in at one door from the darkness out side, flutters through the light and warmth, and passes out through the farther door into the dark unknown beyond. Can this new religion solve for us the mystery? What comes to men after death, in the dark, dim unknown?" If death were the end, then life would indeed be haunted by hopelessness. Faith's answer to such hopelessness is found in the closing words of Psalm 23: "I will dwell in the house of the Lord for ever."

Twelve hours before Jesus was nailed to a cross to die, he said: "In My Father's house are many mansions." (John 14:2) The word *mansion* comes from the Latin verb "manere," meaning to dwell for a time. The late Archbishop of Canterbury William Temple translated Jesus' words, "In My Father house are many resting-places." Temple explained these resting-place are shelters at stages along the road where travelers may rest on their journey. If death were a gate that led to some static state in which there was no future development, then it could really be a boring prison cell! But that isn't what Jesus said about life after death. Instead, he pictured it for us as a great white road leading onward and upward with "resting-places," at each stage of spiritual progress and development, as we venture toward the beatific vision. "If it were not so," said Jesus, "I would have told you!"

60

Means and Ends

America's crucial problem is too many Americans are rich in things and poor in soul. On the one hand, we are rich in things because we have developed great mastery over the means by which we live. These means of living have been made possible by modern technology — all the ways used to produce those goods and services which satisfy our needs and desires. This age of industrial technology started two hundred years ago with the development of power-driven machines. Consider how the means by which we live, made possible by technology, has affected our lives: the automobile has influenced where we live, work, and spend our leisure time; radio and television have changed our entertainment habits; the telephone has revolutionized communications; electric rail lines, huge ocean liners, and supersonic planes have given us "seven-league boots" to travel at great speed. America is the master of the means by which we live!

On the other hand, we are poor in soul because of the unworthy ends for which we live. These ends refer to the purposes and goals that shape our lives. Too often, Americans find themselves "at loose ends," unsettled confused, disordered, because they lack a star worth following. Instead, they are bewitched by shooting stars and run after falling stars, which turn out to be burned-out meteors. General Omar Bradley stated the problem in blunt words, before the Boston Chamber of Commerce on Armistice Day, 1948: "Ours is a world of nuclear giants and ethical infants." Like Old Mother Hubbard, who was unable to give her poor dog a bone, too many Americans, wanting to give their children something worth living for, find their soul's cupboard empty. Never was Jesus more up to date than with this question he once posed: "What will a man gain by winning the whole world at the cost of his true self?" (Matthew 16:26) What profit is there to be rich in the *means* by which we live, yet poor in the *ends* for which we live?

61

Medicine

"Many believers think that to have recourse to science in treating illness is to reject faith," wrote Dr. Paul Tournier. To illustrate this attitude, Dr. Tournier told about a fellow doctor who prescribed a sleeping pill for a patient. The patient told Dr. Tournier: "I take it and it does me good. I am more relaxed, and less nervous, and I work better; and yet I must confess that I never take it without a twinge of conscience. It is as if to use an artificial method were a sign of lack of faith in God."

Does the Bible condemn *medicine?* Or is it a sign of faithlessness to have recourse to medical doctors? About the year 180 B.C., a wise man in Jerusalem named Jesus Ben Sirach wrote a book in the tradition of the Wisdom literature of Israel. This man's grandson, who lived in Egypt, translated the book into Greek. It became part of the Jewish Holy Scriptures in Alexandria, and was called "Ecclesiasticus" or "The Wisdom of Sirach." In that book, the author wrote: "Honor the doctor for his services, for the Lord created him. His skill comes from the Most High . . . The Lord has created medicines from the earth, and a sensible man will not disparage them." (Ecclesiasticus 38:1-4)

Throughout the Bible, various kinds of medicines and external forms of cure are mentioned. For example, when King Hezekiah was sick, God's spokesman, Isaiah, told the King's men to make a plaster from figs, apply it to the boil, and the King recovered. (Isaiah 38:21) Then there was superstitious Naaman who thought God's prophet would not use physical means to cure his leprosy, but Naaman was wrong. (2 Kings 5:11) Remember we pray for daily bread, yet we receive it from the baker! Religion and medicine are meant to cooperate, in the spirit of the French surgeon Ambroise Paré, who said: "I bind up the wounds, but God heals them."

62

Meek

When the Great Fire of London destroyed the original St. Paul's Cathedral in 1666, Sir Christopher Wren, the architect, was commissioned, in 1675, to design and build the new Cathedral. That work took thirty-five long years to complete. When it was finished, in 1710, Queen Anne was invited to see the structure. After she finished looking around, she turned to Sir Christopher and said: "It is awful, it is amusing, and it is artificial." Surprisingly, Wren breathed a sigh of relief. Such is the wonder of words that, in 1710, the word awful meant awe-inspiring; the word amusing meant amazing; and the word artificial meant artistic.

In a similar way, the word meek does not mean, for us, what St. Matthew intended when he reported Jesus' third beatitude: "Blessed are the meek, for they shall inherit the earth." (Matthew 5:5) Behind our English word *meek,* in that text, is the Greek word "praus," which Matthew used when he wrote his account of the Gospel. The word "praus" was used by Greek writers to describe, for instance, the strength and vigor of a wild stallion which has been trained and disciplined. When Jesus talked about the quality of "praus" (translated in Matthew 5:5 as *meek),* he was talking about strength under discipline!

Far from a weak, spineless doormat, the word *meek* in our text refers to a man disciplined in three ways. First, it refers to a man who knows the discipline of being hammered, molded, and shaped by God through long years of hardness. It took God forty years to hammer Moses into shape. Second, it refers to a man who knows the discipline of being harnessed to a great purpose. Jesus was harnessed to the yoke of doing God's will and he offered that yoke to all who follow him. (Matthew 11:29) Third, it refers to a man who knows the discipline of being humbled to a higher Power. In the long run, the earth shall be inherited by people who live under such discipline.

63

Misunderstand

Three children begged for a pet hamster. They promised they would take care of it and, finally, they got one. They named it "Danny." Two months later, when the mother of the children was doing all the cleaning and feeding of the hamster, she found it a prospective new home. When she told the children about Danny's possible new home, she was surprised at how well they took it. One child remarked, "He's been around here a long time — we'll miss him." The mother replied, "Yes, but he's too much work for one person." Another child said, "Maybe if he wouldn't eat so much and wouldn't be so messy, we could keep him." But the mother was firm. "It's time to take Danny to his new home now," she insisted. "Go and get his cage." In tears, the children screamed, "Danny? We misunderstood! We thought that you said, 'Daddy'!"

How common are misunderstandings! The word *misunderstand* comes from two Old English words: "mis" (wrong) and "understandan" (to stand under) To understand is to stand under the place where the object of knowledge stands so you can enter into it and grasp its meaning. To misunderstand is to take a word or an action in the wrong sense, to mistake its meaning. Biography confirms Emerson's conviction that "to be great is to be misunderstood." Moses was misunderstood. St. Luke wrote: "He thought that his own people would understand that God was going to use him to set them free, but they did not understand." (Acts 7:25) Jesus, too, was misunderstood. Some people misunderstood his motives. (Luke 7:34; 11:15) Others misunderstood his message. (John 2:20-21; 11:13) Still others misunderstood his silence before King Herod, at his trial, as a sign of weakness. Even on the cross, Jesus' cry of agony was misunderstood as a cry for Elijah, instead of a cry to God. (Mark 15:35) "Great Spirit," says an Indian prayer, "help me never to judge another until I have walked two weeks in his moccasins!"

64

Motive

A wealthy man had seven married children. He waited for years, but there was never a grandchild. Finally, at Thanksgiving dinner, he announced to his children he had set up a $100,000 trust fund, which would go to the first grandchild. "Now," he said, "let us bow our heads to give thanks for this meal." When he and his wife looked up after the prayer they discovered they were all alone.

The announcement of the trust fund gave this man's children a motive to achieve parenthood quickly. The word *motive* comes from the Latin word "motivus," meaning moving, impelling. A motive is that which moves a person to act. Motives arise from biological drives, social needs, and personal aspirations and goals. The late Dr. Abraham Maslow, a former president of the American Psychological Association, developed a new, comprehensive theory of human motivation called "Third Force Psychology." Dr. Maslow coined that name to distinguish his work, and others, from the two major theories of human behavior, namely Freudianism and Behaviorism.

Dr. Maslow envisioned a human being's primary and growth needs in a hierarchy shaped like a pyramid. At the bottom level of this pyramid are "physiological needs" (air, water, food, shelter, sex) The second level is "safety needs" (an orderly, pre dictable world, adequate salary, good housing). The third level from the bottom is the level of "belongingness and love needs" (to feel loved and wanted). The fourth level is "esteem needs" (both self-respect and esteem from others). The fifth level is "self-actualization" (the desire to become everything one is capable of becoming). At the top of this pyramid of needs that motivate people are "aesthetic needs" (the need to appreciate and to experience beauty).

65

Music

"Next to theology I give to music the highest place and honor. And we see how David and all the saints have wrought their godly thoughts into verse, rhyme, and song." So wrote Martin Luther in tribute to music. The word *music* comes from the Greek word "mousa," meaning a Muse. In Greek mythology, the Muses were a choir of nine sisters who were tha daughters of Jupiter (the father of gods and men) and Mnemosyne, the goddess of memory. Poets and artists would pray to the Muses when they wanted inspiration. The Muses usually dwelt in the mountain glens of Pieria, in east central Greece. It was there that these nine sisters taught Apollo, the god of the sun, about song and music, and about healing. Eventually, Apollo went from being the pupil of the Muses to being their master. According to Greek belief, the poet composed his songs in a kind of divine madness. The Muses were thought to enter the poet and utter poems through him. The poet was an instrument of heaven. "Mousa," the Greek word for Muse, is the root of the word "museum" (temple of the Muses) and music (the art of the Muses).

The Bible contains the words of many Hebrew songs and chants. The book of Psalms, for example, was the hymn book of Israel. Harps, drums, trumpets, cymbals, and other instruments are mentioned in Psalm 150. The Bible traces music to Jubal: "He was the father of all such as handle the harp and organ." (Genesis 4:21, KJV) In the book of Job, music is pictured as present at the creation of the world: "In the dawn of that day the stars sang together, and the heavenly beings shouted for joy." (Job 38:7, TEV)

The power of music can be seen in an incident in King Saul's life. "Whenever the evil spirit . . . came on Saul, David would get his harp and play it. The evil spirit would leave, and Saul would feel better and be all right again." (1 Samuel 16: 23, TEV) Music has power in the family gatherings of home life, in the stirring songs of national life, and in the hymns and anthems of religious life.

66

Mystery

A certain magician worked on a cruise ship between New York City and Bermuda. This magician had a pet parrot who was always ruining his magic act. After the magician made a card disappear, the parrot would say: "He has the card up his sleeve," or, "He slipped it through a hole in his hat." One day there was an explosion in the boiler room and the ship sank. The parrot and the magician found themselves together on a life raft. For three days, the parrot sat silently and stared at the magician. On the third day, the parrot said, "Okay, I give up. What did you do with the ship?"

The disappearance of the ship was a mystery to the parrot. We use the word *mystery* in two ways. First, we use it when we are talking about something hidden, which we can find out if we use our eyes and open our mouths. Sometimes we call a detective story a "murder mystery." When we begin to read the book, we know if the detective-hero will use his eyes and open his mouth to ask the right questions, the mystery will disappear by the last page. Second, we use the word mystery, in its original sense, to mean something hidden, which makes us close our eyes and our mouths in awe when it is revealed. The word mystery comes from the Greek word "musterion," which, in turn, comes from the Greek verb "muein," meaning to close the eyes and the mouth. When believers talk about the mystery of God, they mean God is incomparable. "To whom can God be compared? How can you describe what he is like?" asked Isaiah. (40:18) In a classic analysis of this awe we feel in the presence of God, Rudolf Otto coined the term "mysterium tremendum fascinans," the mystery that is at once overwhelming and fascinating. When I hear the flippancy of some religious people, Blaise Pascal's words come to mind: "I am astonished at the boldness with which people undertake to speak of God."

67

Narcissism

According to Ovid's version of an old Greek legend, a nymph named Liriope was ravaged by a river-god, Cephisus, and gave birth to an extraordinarily beautiful boy named Narcissus. By the time he was sixteen, Narcissus was loved by many others. The nymph Echo, for instance, had fallen deeply in love with him. However, as he treated all who loved him, Narcissus fled from Echo, because he was a cold person incapable of returning love. Echo pined away until, finally, there was nothing left of her except her voice. A rejected suitor prayed to Nemesis, one of the gods, for vengeance on Narcissis, asking, "So may he love and not gain the thing he loves!" Nemesis condemned Narcissus to an appropriate punishment. He was to lie down to drink at a pool, see the reflection of his own beauty, be unable to tear himself away, and die from his self-preoccupation. Even in Hades, the land of the dead, Narcissus continued to gaze at his image in the Stygian pool. He was no longer envied; he was now pitied. The gods were so moved that they transformed his wasted body into a beautiful flower, the Narcissus.

From the name of that Greek character has come the word *narcissism*. Narcissism is often confused with healthy self-love, but there are quite different attitudes toward the self. Narcissism is egocentric, self-centered, and shows lack of concern for other persons. Healthy Christian self-love, on the other hand, is based on God's loving acceptance of us, made known in Jesus of Nazareth. We can rightly love ourselves because God first loved us. Because of divine acceptance, we can, legitimately, value ourselves, discipline ourselves, and, as Jesus commanded, love our neighbor even as we love ourselves. (Luke 10:27)

68

Ostracize

In ancient Greece, a method was developed to handle a dangerous or unpopular citizen considered to be a menace to that state. The citizens would assemble to vote by casting an "ostrakon," a piece of pottery. Those who were in favor of condemning the public menace to leave the country voted by writing the condemned man's name on the ostrakon. From that practice has come our word *ostracize,* meaning to shut out from society, favor, or privileges.

Ostracism is one form of persecution, along with shunning, insults, ridicule, torture, and death. Because we are made to love and be loved, it is most surprising to hear Jesus say, "Happy are those who are persecuted in the cause of right; theirs is the kingdom of heaven." Matthew 5:10)

Why are the persecuted happy? The reason is, as William Barclay reminds us, "persecution is in fact a compliment." It comes only to the person whose life is so positive and real in its effectiveness that society regards that person as a danger. Persecution comes to a person for three reasons. First, he is a rebel to the accepted way. The early Christians were persecuted as "atheists" because they did not worship the accepted gods of the state. Second, he is a rebuke to the conscience of the ungodly. Alcibiades, a wicked young Athenian, said to Socrates: "Socrates, I hate you; for when I am with you I realize what I am." Third, he is a reminder to the wayward of how far they have strayed from the right path. In the book of the Wisdom of Soloman in the Apocrypha, the persecutors of the just man admit the reason for their hatred when they say, "He calls us traitors to our upbringing." (Wisdom of Solomon 2:12) As Nathaniel Howe said, "The way of the world is to praise dead saints and persecute living ones!"

69

Parable

"Truth embodied in a tale shall enter in at lowly doors," wrote Alfred, Lord Tennyson. It is natural for a child to say, "Tell me a story!" That is why Jesus taught through a series of imaginative stories called parables. The word *parable* comes from two Greek words: "para" (beside) and "ballein" (to throw), meaning to create a comparison by throwing one thing down beside something else. A parable is "an earthly story with a heavenly meaning." Unlike allegories, where each detail stands for something, a parable makes only one strong point.

Jesus told parables to show us the nature of the kingdom of God. The word "kingdom" does not signify a place, but a process by which God works out his purpose in our world. In one striking parable, Jesus compared God to a man "looking for fine pearls, and when he finds one that is unusually fine, he goes and sells everything he has, and buys that pearl." (Matthew 13:45)

What is Jesus saying about God in this parable? First, Jesus teaches us that God searches. In other religions, God waits for human beings to climb up to heaven by doing good deeds or by puzzling out the meaning of life on their own. In Jesus, we learn God makes the first move. Second, Jesus teaches us God sets a high value on us. In pre-Christian and post-Christian times, man has been degraded, called a "worm," an "ape," a "cosmic accident." In contrast, says Jesus, God sees each of us as a pearl, something quite valuable. Third, Jesus teaches us God sacrifices himself for us: "He goes and sells everything he has, and buys that pearl." In other religions, human beings offer sacrifices to God. In Jesus Christ, we see that the sacrifice is made by God to reclaim us from the tyrants of sin, sickness, and death which hold us captive.

70

Park

Common words have an uncommon history. Take the word *park,* for example. As a noun, it stands for land set apart for public pleasure. As a verb, it means to leave a vehicle, for a time, in a certain place. Our word *park* comes from the Old French word "parc" which, in turn, came from the Medieval Latin "parricus," meaning an enclosure. Long ago, in what is now France, animals were kept in an enclosure called a "parc." The word was taken to England by William the Conqueror, in 1066, and applied to animal enclosures surrounded by thick hedges. The word "parc" was extended to military encampments, where wagons were used to make an enclosed square, in which cows and horses were turned loose to graze. The wagons and artillery, wheeled into place to form the park, were said to be "parked" there, according to Webb Garrison. To park an automobile now means to leave it by the side of a street or in a lot next to stores. One of the most common signs we see reads, "Don't Park Here!"

Take a good look at life's "Don't Park Here" signs. There are, at least, four areas where it isn't smart to park. First, don't park by your successes. Too often, success can become a sedative luring us to rest on our laurels. Charles Kettering said: "Just the minute you get satisfied with what you've got, the concrete has begun to set in your head." Second, don't park by your setbacks and failures. "This thing we call 'failure' is not the falling down, but the staying down," wrote Mary Pickford. Third don't park by your sorrows. When you park by your sorrows, you let your grief become a grievance so the sorrow in your heart becomes a chip on your shoulder. Fourth, don't park by your spiritual experience. That experience, however grand it might have been, is not meant to be a goal in itself. It is meant to be a gateway to the Great Way of ever increasing knowledge and love, for God and his people of many creeds and colors.

71

Patience

"Where is God's home?" asked the church school teacher of the children seated in front of her. The class was silent for a moment, then a boy named Frankie raised his hand. When the teacher asked Frankie where God's home was, he answered confidently, "In the bathroom at my house!" "Why do you say that?" inquired the shocked teacher. Frankie replied knowingly, "Because every morning my daddy bangs on the bathroom door and says, 'My lord, are you still in there'?"

Frankie's impatient father would grudgingly agree with James, who wrote these words in a New Testament Letter: "When the way is rough, your patience has a chance to grow." (James 1:4) Our English word *patience* comes from a Latin root, "pati," which means to suffer, to endure. Patience is the willingness to put up with waiting, pain, annoyances, troubles, or hurts.

Such patience headed the list of the fifteen characteristics of Christian love, which St. Paul set down in his first letter to the Corinthians. The King James Version of the Bible says such love "suffereth long." When you personalize patience, how it springs to life! God suffereth long and is patient with his wayward children. Again and again, through prophets and sages and the Lord Christ, he has called us to return. Jesus suffers long and is patient with his blundering disciples and followers. The cross shows us the extent of his long-suffering! The disciple of Jesus is called to be as patient and long-suffering toward people as the good Lord has been to us. President Lincoln demonstrated such patience toward Edwin Stanton, one of his severest critics, even making him his Secretary of War. On the night Lincoln was assassinated, Stanton tearfully looked at the President's body and said, "There lies the greatest ruler of men the world has ever seen." The patience of Christ-like love conquered in the end.

72

Pause

When Leonardo da Vinci was painting the scene of Jesus' last supper, on a dining room wall in a certain monastery, he often stood for hours before that wall, pondering his next move. Someone complained to him he wasn't working. Leonardo answered, "When I pause the longest, I make the most telling strokes with my brush." The word *pause* comes from the Greek verb "pauein," meaning to stop. A pause is a short period of inaction, a temporary stop. Someone has said, in music, "pauses are music in the making." There is a momentary rest leading to the production of music more lovely than before. The pause prepares those who are performing and those who are listening for the finer music.

Isn't it possible that the pauses in our lives — those periods of inactivity — may become music in the making? For instance, a period of illness makes us pause and rest awhile. Of course, God doesn't want people to be sick. Jesus made that abundantly clear. Yet, a period of sickness does give us the opportunity to pause and reflect on our priorities. A famous medical doctor, Sir James Crichton Browne, made this insightful comment: "We doctors, in the treatment of nervous diseases, are now constantly compelled to prescribe periods of rest. Some periods are, I think, only Sundays in arrears." How wise and good it is that God gave us one day in seven for worship and rest. How wise of us to observe it regularly!

Young people may resent the fact that disciplined school work makes them pause for awhile before they rush into adult living. Yet that pause can be music in the making! Interruptions make us pause. Though we may resent those interruptions, they can be pauses that jolt our schedules and send us spinning off in new and better directions. No wonder Jesus said to his friends: "Let us go off by ourselves to some place where we will be alone and you can rest awhile." (Mark 6:31)"

73

Pillars of Hercules

Pillars of Hercules was the name ancient Greeks gave to two rocks on either side of the Strait of Gibralter. This Strait is a narrow body of water connecting the Mediterranean Sea and the Atlantic Ocean. The Strait is created by the close proximity of the southernmost part of Spain and the northern coast of Africa. Greek legend said Hercules had placed the rocks on either side of the Strait. The Pillars of Hercules were pictured on the fifteenth century Spanish coats of arms. On the Pillars were scrolls, bearing the Latin words "Ne Plus Ultra" (no more beyond). This was a warning to sailors not to enter the Atlantic Ocean. However, after Christopher Columbus voyaged to the New World and returned, the inscription on the Pillars of Hercules was altered to read "Plus Ultra,' that is, there is something more beyond.

The resurrection of Jesus of Nazareth from the dead brought humanity the assurance that there's something more beyond. Reflecting on the meaning of Jesus' victory over death, St. Paul wrote this: "Our present earthly body is like a tent in which a man lives temporarily while he is on a journey from one place to another. But we know that, if this temporary home is demolished, we have a house which God will give us, a house not built by any human hands, made to last in heaven for ever." (1 Corinthians 5:1, Barclay translation) President John Quincy Adams shared that faith. Alvin Rogness reports that, when Adams was eighty-one years old, a friend inquired of his health. Adams replied: "John Adams is very well, thank you. But the tenement he has inhabited these many years is in a sad state of disrepair. It sags in the corners, its roof leaks, and when the wind blows it creaks and groans in every joint. I suspect that John Adams will soon be forced to seek other quarters. But John Adams himself is very well, thank you." Every Sunday is a little Easter reminding us planet Earth bears as "chief treasure one forsaken grave" across which faith sees the inscription, "Plus Ultra" — more beyond!

74

Poor

"Blessed are the poor in spirit: for theirs is the kingdom of heaven," said Jesus. This is the first of an eight-verse prose poem called "The Beatitudes." In each of these eight "be-attitudes," the word "blessed" stands for the happiness which will come to you if you live by these amazing attitudes of being. The word Jesus used for *poor* is, in the Greek New Testament, the word "ptochos," meaning absolute poverty. Involuntary economic poverty is not being advocated by Jesus as a virtue. What Jesus is telling us is personal happiness begins when we recognize our needs and have the humility to admit our poverty of spirit. What is the significance of our needs? Our sense of need is not a sign of weakness. It is a badge of our dignity, a sign of our greatness. Needs indicate where a creature is, on the scale of existence. Rocks have no needs. Plants need water and chemicals. Amoeba need food. Savages need only a straw hut and raw food to satisfy them. Man, at his highest, needs music, books, art, companionship, meaning, and answers to satisfy his intellect.

How do we become aware of our needs? First, the problems of life make demands on us that produce a sense of inadequacy. Who can face life's demands without recognizing the need for spiritual reinforcement to meet the strain? Second, the prodigal actions of life, by ourselves and others, make us aware of moral failure. Sin produces the steel bands of habit, the haunting ghosts of guilt, and the bitter banquet of consequences. Moral failure and its aftermath make us aware of our need for divine forgiveness and a fresh start. Third, the possibilities of life give us a vision of what could be, and awaken our sense of need for courage, commitment and clear thinking. Happiness begins when a person recognizes his needs, becomes open-minded, and is willing to learn.

75

Possibilities

"You are a promise, you are a possibility," sang the children in our Vacation Church School last summer. However, three factors give us a problem in accepting such good news about ourselves. First, we have bad memories of our past performances. Because of failures, guilt, and wrong choices, we find the good news about our *possibilities* too good to to be true. Second, we see the negatives in our present situation. As our health declines, our age advances, and our energies run down, we don't feel full of promise. Third, the fear of failure, in our future prospects, paralyzes our initiative. This fear makes us play it safe so we can avoid losing our self-esteem.

As you face tomorrow, consider the theological reasons why you can believe in your possibilities. First, God as Creator has filled every created thing with possibilities. Years ago, a box was found in Palestine. In that box were seeds twenty centuries old. When planted, those seeds showed they were still filled with the potential to become plants. The acorn is a potential oak tree. The oak tree is a potential church pew. Second, God as Liberator has a well-documented record of finding great possibilities in unlikely places. In a band of Hebrew slaves shut up in Egypt, God saw the potential of a great nation, Israel, which would be his chosen instrument for educating mankind about himself. In weak, undependable Simon bar Jonah, the God-man, Jesus Christ, saw the possibilities of a man of faith whom he nicknamed "Rocky" (Peter). On such men of faith is the church built! In a novel by Lloyd Douglas, Jesus asked Zacchaeus, "What did you see that made you desire this peace?" Zacchaeus replied, "Good Master, I saw — mirrored in your eyes — the face of the Zacchaeus I could become." In Christ's eyes, you will see the person you can become.

76

Prepare

Long ago and far away there lived a court jester named Giacomo. Because of his great ability to make people laugh, he became the favorite of the king. On one occasion, the king was so impressed by the jester's talent, he gave him a golden staff and proclaimed, "Giacomo, you are the world's greatest fool." Many years passed and one day the jester was summoned to the bedside of the king, who lay sick and dying. Looking up at Giacomo, the king said, "I feel that I soon will be taking a long trip and I won't be coming back." The jester replied, "Is your majesty prepared for this journey and are you ready for what lies ahead?" The king answered, "No." Giacomo laid the golden staff on the bed and said, "I give you back this staff which you gave to me so many years ago. I believe that for you to go from one world into another unprepared makes you a greater fool than I."

One way to *prepare* for death is to practice dying now. Morton Kelsey, an Episcopal priest, gives us a clue with these words from his recent book *Afterlife:* "One's ego must die to make room for a new center of being which is given." Thirty years ago, a Roman Catholic priest, Fulton J. Sheen, made a similar distinction between the ego and the I. The ego is our superficial self, formed by our mistaken conformity to the spirit of this world. The I, on the other hand, is our personality, made in the image of God. "As the ego dies, the I is born," wrote Sheen. Unless we practive putting the ego to death, by detaching ourselves from things and disciplining our evil inclinations, we shall be as unready for death as the unprepared king. That's why Jesus asked: "What will a man gain by winning the whole world, at the cost of his true self?" (Luke 9:25)

77

Problem

"I'm the head of my house," announced one recently-married husband to another. "After all, I should be. I'm the one who earns the money." The other man replied, "My wife and I have a different arrangement. We've agreed that I should decide all the major problems and she handles the minor ones. Would you believe that not one problem of major importance has come up in the last six months!"

The word *problem,* which confronts us everywhere today, comes from two Greek words, "pro" (forward) and "ballein" (to throw). Problems are difficulties to face, puzzles to solve, questions to answer, that are thrown across our path. There are three ways you can tackle your problems. First, expect problems. Even Jesus was not immune to problems. He had to cope with the misunderstanding of the crowds (John 10:20), the hostility of the authorities (Mark 3:6), and the defection of followers (John 6:66).

Second, inspect problems. Confronting problems is the essence of our daily lives. Tough as they are, problems are good for us, because we become stronger as we wrestle with them. Inspect your problems carefully, then, remembering the words of two smart men. Henry Kaiser said: "A problem is only an opportunity in work clothes." Stanley Arnold advised: "Every problem contains the seeds of its own solution."

Third, disrespect problems. When you've looked them over, then overlook them, see beyond them. That's what Jesus had in mind when he told the story about the farmer who scattered seed. (Matthew 13:1-9) In spite of the difficulties the farmer faced, the power of God was in that seed. Therefore, the victory of a rich harvest was assured. Because every problem has a limited life span, the frustrations will, in God's good time, give way to fruitfulness.

78

Procastinate

When I was a boy, I met Connie Mack at old Shibe Park. Mack served as the owner-manager of the Philadelphia Athletics baseball team from 1901 until he retired in 1950. He once said: "Since I couldn't be sure of controlling myself and my tongue immediately after a defeat, I made it a rule never to see the players right after a defeat. I wouldn't discuss the defeat with them until the next day. By that time, I had cooled off, the mistakes didn't loom so large, and I could talk things over calmly and the men wouldn't get angry and try to defend themselves." I call that an example of positive procrastination. The word *procrastinate* comes from two Latin words, "pro" (forward) and "cras" (tomorrow). To procrastinate is to put things off until tomorrow. Negative procrastination was condemned by Benjamin Franklin who said: "Never put off till tomorrow that which you can do today." It certainly applies to such matters as paying your income tax, buying a birthday present, and handing in a paper for school.

In one of his memorable parables, however, Jesus advocated a positive procrastination. "The reign of God," he said, "is like a farmer sowing good seed in his field." (Matthew 13:24) One night, as the farmer slept, his enemy came and sowed weeds among the wheat. What a simple, yet accurate, picture Jesus drew of what life is really like: good and evil intermingled in every person, movement, and institution. The farmer's men said, "Sir, it was good seed you sowed in your field; where did the weeds come from?" "It was some enemy who did this," replied the farmer. Not everything that happens, in God's world, is God's ideal purpose. Beside the Divine Sower, a shadowy Enemy is at work. "Do you want us to go and pull up the weeds?" asked the men. "No," the farmer answered. Instead, practice positive procrastination, to avoid doing more harm than good by hasty and premature actions.

79

Pure

When the English poet Alfred, Lord Tennyson was in old age, he asked his son, who was to be the executor of his estate, to see that the publishers of his poems put the poem "Crossing the Bar" at the end of the book. We do not know why Tennyson made that request. But we should note, when he was once asked what was his dearest wish, he answered, "A clearer vision of God." This may be why he specified his collection of poems end with one in which he said, "I hope to see my Pilot face to face when I have crossed the bar." This vision of God, the goal of humanity, is addressed by Jesus, when he said, "Blessed are the pure in heart, for they shall see God." (Matthew 5:8) The Greek word for *pure,* in this text, is "katharos," which has the basic meaning of unmixed, unadulterated, unalloyed. Unmixed milk or wine, unalloyed silver, wheat cleansed of chaff is "katharos," genuine, sincere. As Dr. Moffatt once translated this text, "Blessed are they who are not double-minded . . . " What you see depends on what you be!

The single-minded, wholehearted person, said Jesus, will see God. This seeing is a matter of mental insight. When the prophet Isaiah described the vision he had, while at worship in the Jerusalem Temple (Isaiah 6:1-8), he showed us what it means to see God. First, to see God means confrontation of the mystery of God. The word "God" is an inadequate symbol for the awesomeness of that Ultimate Reality behind, and prior to, this created universe. Second, to see God means consolation by the mercy of God, whose forgiveness cleanses us of our sense of inadequacy and unworthiness. Third, to see God means making a contribution to the mission of God. That mission expresses God's will and good purpose, which is always for human well-being, health, and happiness.

80

Rainbow

When people have been brought through the seriousness of a great illness and then reflect on their life, they often rise from the sickness with two feelings. On the one hand, they feel God is calling them to a fresh start. On the other hand, they are haunted by the fear that the illness may return. Such must have been the experience of Noah, when he stepped out of the ark. Every cloud bank and fresh drop of rain made Noah feel insecure and afraid. To encourage Noah, God made a mutual agreement with him called a covenant. The sign of this divine encouragement is the *rainbow:* "My bow," says God, "I set in the cloud, sign of the covenant between myself and earth. When I cloud the sky over the earth, the bow shall be seen in the clouds." (Genesis 9:13-14)

The rainbow set in the clouds teaches us three lessons. First, it teaches us to find the favorable in the fearful. In the mid-1800's Henri Dunant found, in the fearful clouds of the Austrian-Sardinian War, a most favorable inspiration: the idea of an international organization, to care for the wounded. For a symbol of this organization he reversed the Swiss flag and produced a Red Cross on a white background. Second, the rainbow in the clouds teaches us to find the meaningful in the mysterious. Clouds are symbolic of life's mysteries, yet, on those clouds, God has set his rainbow to encourage us to detect meaning in the mysterious. Third, it teaches us to find the changeless in the changing. Of all the changing things in the world, clouds are among the most changing. When God set the rainbow in the clouds, he reminded us there are fixed stars in this changing world, stars by which we can steer safely through life. As Archibald Rutledge wrote: "It takes solitude, under the stars, for us to be reminded of our eternal origin and our far destiny."

81

Reckon

"Man of La Mancha" is the musical adaptation of Miguel de Cervantes' novel, *Don Quixote,* written between 1605 and 1615. It is the story of an aged idealist and his comrade, Sancho Panza, who set out on a campaign to restore the age of chivalry, to battle evil, and right all wrongs. When Don Quixote arrived at a roadside inn, he envisioned a serving-girl and prostitute, named Aldonza, as his ideal woman, whom he called Dulcinea. Raped, disillusioned, and angered, Aldonza screamed at him, "Oh, don't call me a lady. I'm only a kitchen slut reeking with sweat. A strumpet men use and forget . . . I'm only Aldonza. I am nothing at all!" Nevertheless, because he considered and treated her as a person of genuine value, Don Quixote's constant affirmations succeeded in transforming Aldonza into Dulcinea, the fine person he believed her to be.

What Don Quixote did to Aldonza is the opposite of the slang expression, to bad-mouth. That phrase means to talk badly about, to criticize or malign. Instead of bad-mouthing her, he good-mouthed her; he regarded her and treated her as good and upright, a person of wholesomeness and integrity. Bishop FitzSimons Allison, of the Episcopal Church, has written: "Every enterprise I know that frees people from hang-ups — from Alcoholics Anonymous to group therapy — is at bottom an attempt to good-word a person, enabling him to accept himself by being accepted . . ." The New Testament Greek word for this good-mouthing is *logidzomai,* meaning to regard and treat as good. This word appears in Paul's letter to the Christians in Rome as *reckon:* "Reckon yourselves as dead unto sin." (Romans 6:11) *Reckon* means to consider as being of a specific value. We can good-mouth ourselves because God has reckoned us to be good and acceptable, in company with Jesus Christ. That is the Good News of the Christian message.

82

Repent

A member of the Episcopal Church approached her priest and said, “Father, my dog died this morning and I want to know if you think it is all right to have a funeral for him. He was just like a member of my family.” The priest, somewhat taken aback by this strange request, said, “Yes, I suppose it would be appropriate.” The grieving woman replied, “Father, who do I get to have the funeral?” Not at all pleased with the thought of having a funeral for a dog, the priest answered, “I have a very busy day tomorrow. Try the Baptist minister. Perhaps he can help you.” The woman, said, “Thank you, Father, but how much should I pay the Baptist minister — $200 or $300?” The eyes of the priest lit up, he put his arms around the woman and said, “Why, my dear lady, why didn't you tell me it was an Episcopal dog?”

The priest's change of mind illustrates what we mean by the word *repent.* It comes from the Greek word *metanoo,* which, in turn, comes from *meta* (change) and *nous* (mind). To *repent* means to change your outlook and attitude, to reverse your former judgment, to reorient your life. Jesus' first words, as he appeared on the stage of history, were about repentance and faith: “ ‘The appointed time has come,’ he said. ‘the Kingdom of God is almost here. Repent and believe that the Good News is true’.” (Mark 1:15).

Repentance has two aspects; one negative and one positive. The negative aspect of repentance has to do with the past. You realize you've been traveling down the wrong road, headed in the wrong direction. The positive aspect of repentance has to do with the future. You turn around, change the direction you have been traveling, and walk a new way. The stimulus to repent seldom comes from inside us. Usually it comes from outside us, as we catch a vision of how good, genuine, beautiful, and healthy life can be, when it is lived in God's way! The glory of Christ is not simply that he brings forgiveness to those who repent. It is that his radiant life brings repentance to those who need it.

83

Resurrection

In 1908, near La Chapelle-aux-Saints, France, a human body was discovered in a cave. These human remains were 50,000 years old. A noted American anthropologist, Loren Eisley, commented about these ancient remains at a scientific symposium: "Massive flint-hardened hands had shaped a sepulcher, and placed flat stones to guard the dead man's head. A haunch of meat had been left to aid the dead man's journey. Worked flints, a little treasure of the human dawn, had been poured lovingly into the grave. And down the untold centuries the message had come without words: 'We too were human, we too suffered, we too believed that the grave is not the end. We too whose faces affright you now, knew human agony and human love'."

That unspoken message, from a cave in France, tells us our loves and our hopes as humans are far older than we ever realized. And a cave outside Jerusalem has confirmed and transformed that ancient yearning to conquer death. To that empty cave, the forsaken grave in the garden of Joseph of Arimathea, we look again every Sunday. Every Sunday is a little Easter. We hear again, by the silent witness of the church's existence, the message about Jesus' resurrection. Peter, the big fisherman, testified: "God raised him, releasing him from the pangs of death." (Acts 2:24) Remember both the word *resurrection* and the term *raising* are metaphors, visual images, picture words taken from "awakening" and "rising" from sleep. Resurrection is like returning to consciousness from sleep. But it is also unlike it. It is transformation to a new, unparalleled, immortal life. Jesus died. He passed to the realm of the dead, and he returned to walk in newness of life. Paul wrote: "Christ has broken the power of death and brought life and immortality to light through the Gospel." (2 Timothy 1:10)

84

Seeds

A group of ministers and a salesmen's organization were holding conventions in the same hotel. The catering department had to work at top speed, serving dinners to both groups. The salesmen were having "Spiked Watermelon" for dessert. But the overworked chef discovered this alcoholic tidbit was being served to the ministers, by mistake. "Quick," he commanded a waiter, "if they haven't eaten the watermelon, bring it back and we'll give it to the salesmen." The waiter returned, in a minute, and reported that it was too late — the ministers were eating the liquor-spiced dessert. "Well," demanded the excited chef, "what did they say? How did they like it?" The waiter replied, "I don't know how they liked it, but they're dividing up the seeds and putting them in their pockets."

Why were those ministers so anxious to save those *seeds?* Maybe they thought they could raise "Spiked Watermelon"! But one thing is sure: they saved those seeds because they had learned an important lesson from Christ. Our Lord once said, "How can I describe the Kingdom of God? It is like a tiny mustard seed! Though this is one of the smallest of seeds, yet it grows to become one of the largest of plants." (Mark 4:30) See what this means for you right now! First, it means there are infinite possibilities in little beginnings, if God is in them. Out of that little town of Bethlehem came one solitary life, which has divided history into "before Christ" and "in the year of our Lord"! Second, all the flowers of our tomorrows are in the seeds of today. Plant your seeds where you are and you'll bloom where you're planted. That's why Sunday worship is so important. At worship, God is sowing his power-packed seed-thoughts into our minds. Visualize these words over your church door: "This is a magic place! We are making our tomorrows by God's grace!"

85

Shadow

In the lands of the East, a person's *shawdow* has greater significance than in our scientifically oriented West. In India, for example, a member of the highest caste, the Brahman, would throw away his food if the shadow of an untouchable, India's lowest caste, passed over that food. The shadow of some people was thought to be contaminated. On the other hand, when Mahatma Gandhi lived there, people would maneuver themselves so Gandhi's shadow would fall on them and bring them blessing. In the days after Jesus' return to life that same belief was at work. St. Luke tells us "sick people were carried out into the streets and placed on beds and mats so that at least Peter's sh so Gandhi's shadow would fall on them and bring them blessing. In the days after Jesus' return to life that same belief was at work. St. Luke tells us "sick people were carried out into the streets and placed on beds and mats so that at least Peter's shadow might fall on some of them as he passed by."(Acts 5:15) The word *shadow* comes from the Old English word sceadwe, meaning shade, the darkness which something casts on a surface by intercepting direct rays of light.

If you insist on taking the Bible literally at this point, then you'll have to defend an ancient superstition. However, if you can approach this passage seriously, but not literally, then you have an example of a profoundly important psychological fact. Each one of us does cast some kind of shadow of influence, either good or bad. Like the ripples caused by a stone thrown into a swimming pool, your influence ripples out of you like a shadow. Consider how Jesus' influence has fallen across the centuries through the ancient institution we call the Christian church, and you'll see the truth in Ralph Waldo Emerson's words: "An institution is the lengthened shadow of one man." Nearly 3,000 years ago, Isaiah wrote: the influence of a good man was as refreshing "as a cooling shadow of a mighty rock within a hot and weary land."(Isaiah 32:2) Become conscious, therefore, of the powerful, unconscious shadow of influence which you exercise on others daily.

86

Shalom

Shalom is a beautiful and melodic Hebrew word which comes from the root "slm" signifying wholeness, health, and harmony. Shalom is usually translated into English as peace. In modern English, however, peace is often understood negatively as the absence of open conflict. In Hebrew, shalom is an intensely positive word about everything a person needs for a full, complete life: health, harmonious relationships, and human fulfillment. In the seventh beatitude, in his Sermon on the Mount, Jesus said: "Blessed are the peacemakers, for they shall be called the sons of God." (Matthew 5:9) No doubt Jesus had in mind the rich meaning of that word shalom when he spoke of peacemakers.

Those who are active, energetic workers for shalom do so in three areas. First, there is shalom within a person. Note the author of Psalm 122 equated peace with prosperity, when he wrote in Hebrew parallelism: "Peace be within your ramparts and prosperity in your palaces." Jesus healed a chronically ill woman and sent her away by saying, "Go into peace," or, more clearly, "Go and enjoy your new health." (Mark 5:34, William Barclay translation) All who work for human well-being are peacemakers. Second, there is shalom between persons. Jesus encouraged good human relationships when he said, "Live in peace with one another." (Mark 9:50) As Barclay has written: "The man who divides men is doing the devil's work; the man who unites men is doing God's work." Third, there is shalom towards persons from "God, our source of peace." (Romans 15:33) At Bethlehem, angels heralded Jesus' birth as the sign, on earth, of God's shalom. As the New English Bible renders their song: "Glory to God in highest heaven, and on earth his peace, his favor towards men." (Luke 2:14)

87

Star Trek

"Star Trek III: The Search for Spock" is the third motion picture to grow out of the television series, originally shown from 1966 to 1969 and then cancelled for lack of viewers. I have followed, enthusiastically, the adventures of James Kirk, master of the USS Enterprise, Science Officer Spock, and the Ship's surgeon, Dr. Leonard "Bones" McCoy, along with the rest of the crew on the bridge. One reason I have enjoyed *Star Trek* is because it challenges me to face the difficulties that the show raises for religion.

The first difficulty *"Star Trek"* raises, for religion, is the size of the universe. The vastness of the physical universe seems to dwarf man into insignificance. Modern telescopes reveal to us hundreds of millions of stars. What, indeed, is man that some God should be mindful of him? Then I realized I could balance the "terror" of the telescope through the marvel of the microscope. It shows us the Power that made the stars is equally careful about things too small to be seen. Size doesn't determine value. Small as they are, diamonds and babies are dear to us! The second difficulty *Star Trek* raises, for religion, is the matter of numbers. The countless multitudes of living beings in space make it hard for us to imagine God cares for one individual. But doesn't greater knowledge go hand in hand with care about the parts that make up the whole? A good librarian isn't overwhelmed by shelves of books; she knows and cares about each one. Is God less knowledgeable about his creatures? The third difficulty *Star Trek* raises is the question of purpose. Can the Power that created the vast expanse of interstellar space, galaxies, suns, and the planets in their courses, have a purpose that includes man? When doubters say, "Astronomically speaking, man is insignificant," Faith answers, "Astronomically speaking, man is the astronomer!"

88

Stars

In a small monastery there was a little monk who was extremely shy. He lived in terror of the day when the abbot would say to him, "Tomorrow you preach in chapel." Sure enough, the day came when the abbot scheduled him to preach. The little monk mounted the pulpit and said, "Do you know what I'm about to say?" The assembled monks shook their heads, "No." The little monk announced, "Neither do I. The service is ended. Go in peace." The disappointed abbot rescheduled the little monk to preach the next morning. Again he stepped into the pulpit and asked, "Do you know what I'm about to say?" To encourage him all the monks nodded, "Yes." The little monk said, "Well, if you all know what I'm going to say, there's no reason for me to say it. The service is ended. Go in peace." The angry abbot scolded him and said, "Tomorrow is your last chance!" The next morning the little monk looked down from the pulpit and asked, "Do you know what I'm about to say?" Some of the monks shook their heads yes and some shook their heads no. They thought they had the little monk cornered. But he said, "Well, then, will those of you who know what I am about to say kindly tell those who don't know. The service is ended. Go in peace."

Why was the little monk so hesitant about preaching? Perhaps he was afraid that he would fail. Perhaps he feared failing because it would lower his sense of self-worth. Whatever the reason, the paralysis of perfectionism prevented him from allowing the light and warmth of truth to shine through his personality. Writing to friends at Philippi about their contemporaries, St. Paul said, "You must shine among them like stars lighting up the sky." (Philippians 2:15) We are called to be *stars,* not in the theatrical sense, but in the personal sense. The stars in the human family are those people who shine like bright lights in the dark nights, offering cheer, comfort, and hope.

89

Stars and Sorrows

"The Lord . . . heals the brokenhearted and binds up their wounds. He counts the number of the stars and calls them all by their names." (Psalm 147:3-4) Isn't that a surprising combination of God's attributes? Side by side are placed his active pity, in the small circles of human experience, and his unmeasured power, in the great realms of the natural world. Can there really be any connection between the starry heavens above and the suffering hearts below? Yes, there's an underlying relationship between *stars and sorrows* which points to the care of God. Heaven with its glories is close to earth with its griefs. Heaven with its holiness is always touching earth with its heartbreaks. The God of the stars above is also the God of the scars below.

How are stars and sorrows linked? For one thing, both are the common possession of all men. No one has a monopoly on the starlit heavens; stars are the possession of poor and rich alike. Likewise, the sorest heartbreaks are the heritage of all sorts and conditions of men, because no one is exempt from the human experience of being crushed, wounded, and broken. Second, both stars and heartaches make us realize our littleness and feebleness. There is nothing which can make you feel so tiny and powerless as the sight of the sky on a clear night, nothing except the heartbreaks of life. Third, millions of the stars are hidden from our sight despite our strongest telescopes. Isn't that how it is with so many of our unseen hurts? They, too, are hidden from the sight of others. In 1816, the Irish poet, Thomas Moore, writing in Virginia, penned a poem which has become a hymn. In it he says: "Here bring your wounded hearts, here tell your anguish; Earth has no sorrow that heaven cannot heal."

90

Stars and Stables

In 1899, a boy named Jeno was born in Budapest, Hungary. Jeno's father, a Budapest dentist, named him after Jeno Hubay, a great violinist of that time. Jeno's musical talent quickly became obvious. At age two, he could identify symphonies. At three, he was playing a tiny custom-made violin. When his parents took him to a violin recital at age four, he shocked the audience by announcing to a certain violinist, "You played an F-sharp instead of an F." Jeno was admitted to the Royal Academy of Music in Budapest when he was five, first performed publicly at ten and was a professor of music at sixteen.

Jeno was twenty-one when he was lured to the United States by promises from a manager whose words were false. Jeno had followed his "star" until it came to stand over a "stable," an unpromising place in the shape of a movie theater. "It seemed a bitter end to my young dreams," he said, "but it was training of the most valuable kind." From that stable-like experience, at the Capital Theater in New York, Eugene Ormandy rose to concertmaster, then conductor of the eighty-five-piece orchestra. In the mid 1930's, he became the director of the Philadelphia Orchestra, where he served until his death.

Eugene Ormandy's story reminds us again that life is made up of *stars and stables.* A *star* is a symbol of some dream we follow. A *stable* is the down-to-earth embodiment of that dream. For example, a young man sees the star of medicine rise in his sky, and he follows it until it comes to stand over a stable — a poorly-managed hospital where the administration and his peers cut corners. Or, a young girl sees the star of romance rise in her sky, and she follows it into marriage, until it comes to stand over a sink full of dishes, a hamper full of clothes, and a roomful of children. Sooner or later, every star comes to stand over a stable. Blessed are those dedicated and resilient people who can live in that invigorating tension between stars and stables.

91

Stone Soup

Do you know how to make *stone soup?* Three hungry soldiers came to a village where they asked for food. The villagers claimed to have no food. One of the soldiers said, "We'll have to make some 'stone soup'." The soldiers got a huge kettle, filled it with water, and built a fire under the kettle. The curious villagers gathered around and watched, as a soldier selected a flat, smooth stone and dropped it into the bubbling water. After a minute, he took a spoon and tasted the stone soup. "Wonderful." he said, "but it needs some salt." Two children disappeared and soon returned with salt and pepper. "It sure smells good," said another soldier, "but a little cabbage would make it better." A woman ran home and returned with a cabbage. Item by item, the soldiers told the villagers what would make the Stone Soup better: a few carrots, celery, turnips, potatoes, some onion. One by one, the items were brought. Finally, the soldiers announced that a piece of roast beef would add a delicious final touch. A family donated the roast beef. Tables and chairs were set up in the center of the village, torches lit, and the people ate amidst music, laughter, and the joyous shouts of children.

Do you see what the soldiers did? They acted with optimism and enthusiasm. They gave those villagers an opportunity to share what they had. Individually, those people didn't have enough to do the job. But, when they had a chance to work together, they generously shared their provisions. As Burton Hillis wrote: "If there's a stranger in your neighborhood today, better check up on him; he may need a friend. If he's still a stranger tomorrow, better check up on your neighborhood.

92

Thanksgiving Letters

During the Depression of the 1930's, Dr. William L. Stidger and some friends found themselves, on Thanksgiving Eve, talking about banks closing, people out of work, and salaries going down. It was a pretty gloomy conversation. "There sure isn't much to be thankful for," said one friend. Finally, Bill Stidger had enough. He looked around the group, then said: "Well, I, for one, am grateful to Mrs. Wendt." Bill went on to explain that Mrs. Wendt was an old schoolteacher who had gone out of her way to introduce him to the poetry of Alfred, Lord Tennyson. "Did you ever thank her?" some one asked. Dr. Stidger admitted he never had. That evening he sat down and wrote a letter to Mrs. Wendt. A few weeks later came a reply written in the uncertain scrawl of an aged woman: "My Dear Willie: . . . I want you to know what your note meant to me. I am an old lady in my eighties, living alone in a small room, cooking my own meals, lonely and seeming like the last leaf on the tree . . . You will be interested to know, Willie, that I taught school for fifty years and in all that time yours is the first letter of appreciation I have ever received. It came on a blue, cold morning, and it cheered my lonely old heart as nothing has cheered me in many years."

When Dr. Stidger finished reading that simple, sincere note from one of his teachers of long ago, he wept. And he resolved to continue writing these *Thanksgiving letters,* as he called them, every November. After ten years of writing these letters, Dr. Stidger reflected: "I never dreamed the response would be so satisfying. I had merely thought of building up in myself an attitude of gratitude such as my friend suggested that night." For several years, I have made this same suggestion to my congregation on Thanksgiving Eve: take time on Thanksgiving Day to write a brief note to people who have contributed something definite and lasting in your life. You can do so much good with a pen, an envelope, a stamp, and good will!

93

The Existence of God

Robinson Crusoe is an imaginary story about a sailor, who was marooned on a desert island. One day, Crusoe saw, in the sand, a footprint that was not his own. From the existence of that footprint, Crusoe reasoned there was another person on the island. Finding out what the other person was like had to wait until they met, and the other revealed himself to Crusoe.

In a similar way, human beings have reasoned that One they have called God exists, because they have seen his footprint, as it were, in the order and power of the world around them. In 1957, the world's most complicated astronomical clock was exhibited in the Town Hall of Copenhagen. The clock had ten faces, fifteen thousand parts, and was accurate to two-fifths of a second in three hundred years. Yet, that clock had to be regulated by a more precise clock, the universe itself. If the clock in Copenhagen had a maker, how much more the clock of the universe with its billions of moving parts, from atoms to stars?

Another reason men have detected *the existence of God* is because of evolution in the universe. Merely stretching out the creative process from six days to eighteen billion years doesn't eliminate the need of a first cause. To think otherwise is like saying if the handle of a brush were long enough, it would paint by itself!

Still another reason people believe God exists is because of the correspondence between our needs and their fulfillment. The eye needs light and there is light. The ear is made for sound and the environment meets that need. The body hungers for food and sexual gratification and those hungers do have their fulfillment. Is it unreasonable, therefore, to hold that mankind's ancient need for God points to a cosmic companion who can fulfill that longing? It seemed perfectly sensible to an early Christian to write: "Every house . . . is built by someone — and God is the one who has built all things." (Hebrews 3:4)

94

Through

"Keep my lad safe, O Lord. Hide him under Thy wings. The bullet was never made that can pierce Thy wings." That prayer, uttered by a father for his son in World War I, was recalled by English pastor, Dr. Leslie Weatherhead, who added this comment: "But the boy was shot through the head." There are passages in the Old Testament where religion is viewed as an insurance policy against calamity. Wily old Jacob, for example, tried to strike such a bargain with God: "If you will be with me and protect me on the journey I am making and give me food and clothing, and if I return safely to my father's house, then you will be my God." (Genesis 28:20-21) There are texts in the Psalms encouraging the same illusion. (Psalm 17: 8; 27:5; 91:3-13) "Hundreds of people have never progressed in their thinking beyond the psalmists I have quoted," wrote Dr. Weatherhead, "and if they lose a child or their health or their loved one, they think God has let them down."

Of course, we fear life's shadowed experiences. Mature faith, however, is not based on the preposition "out of," but on the word "through." "Yea, though I walk through the valley of the shadow of death, I will fear no evil, for thou art with me." (Psalm 23:4) The word *through* comes from an Indo-European base, "ter," meaning in one side and out the other. "Ter" passed into Latin as "trans," across. Mature faith does not look upon religion as an insurance policy against calamity, but as the assurance that when we have to go through those gloomy times, God will be there, too. Isaiah of Babylon gives us this word from God: "When you pass through deep waters, I will be with you." (Isaiah 43:2) Modern Christians need to remember the major symbol of faith is not a couch to which we can escape from tough times, but a cross rooted deeply in the dark, bloody soil of painful human experiences.

95

Tired

In the entrance hall of Johns Hopkins Hospital in Baltimore is a remarkable statue of Jesus of Nazareth. He is portrayed as The Great Physician. His face is strong, yet tender. His arms are extended, in welcome, to all persons who enter that sanctuary of healing. At the base of the statue are these words of Jesus: "Come to me, all of you who are tired from carrying heavy loads, and I will give you rest." (Matthew 11:28)

The word *tired* comes from the Old English word "tiorian," meaning to fail, to become weak, to cease. Faith's answer to tiredness is found in the Psalmist's affirmation about God: "Thou preparest a table before me in the presence of mine enemies; Thou anointest my head with oil; my cup runneth over." (Psalm 23:5) God has a threefold prescription for tiredness.

First, let up from activity. Give nature regular periods of rest, and the body will throw off the fatigue toxins. To cease from labor is the meaning of the Hebrew word passed into English as Sabbath.

Second, let go of your problem. Often, it is the mind that makes the body tired, because it has the problem of no goal or too many goals. Monkeys in Java love a certain local red bean. To capture these monkeys, the natives take coconuts, hollow them out, leaving only a two-inch diameter hole. They rope the coconut to a tree, put a red bean inside, and wait. When a monkey reaches inside the coconut and grabs the red bean, his fist won't fit back through the hole. No monkey ever lets go of the bean, in order to get away. Though we say we're gripped by some problem, often we are the ones who are doing the holding on. Let go!

Third, let in outside power. We don't nourish ourselves, but are dependent on the plant and animal world. From outside us comes air for our lungs and light for our eyes. Likewise, our spirits can be nourished by the larger spiritual world. Feed your mind with positive companionships!

96

Tomato

Before 1830, tomatoes were known as love apples. English knights, in earlier centuries, gave tomatoes to their sweethearts as special favors. Sir Walter Raleigh is said to have given one to Queen Elizabeth. The tomato was domesticated by the Indians of Central America. Our word *tomato* comes from those Central American Indians who called it "tomatl." The tomato spread to both North and South America before Christopher Columbus arrived in the New World. Seeds of the tomato were taken to Europe, where the plant was raised for decoration. Because a superstition arose that the tomato stimulated love, it gained the name love apple. Although it was native to America, it was eaten in Europe long before people in the United States used it for food. People here considered it poisonous.

On September 26, 1830, a tomato farmer named Colonel Robert Johnson from Salem, New Jersey, announced he would eat an entire basket of them. As Johnson ate his first tomato, a band played and people fainted. He finished the basketful, as the astonished crowd watched. The courage of Colonel Johnson reminds us of Frank Tyger's words: "The road to success is usually off the beaten path." Beaten paths are for beaten men! The heroes of our religious tradition didn't use their faith as an escape, but as an energetic and courageous adventure into the unknown. At the beginning of Israel's history, for example, is Abraham who left the beaten path of life in Ur "without knowing where he was going." (Hebrews 11:8) Jesus of Nazareth left the beaten path of the old religion by doubting his ancestors' traditional wisdom. (Matthew 5:21f) St. Paul left the beaten path of Judaism. What insight and courage it took for him to write: "We know that a person is put right with God only through faith in Jesus Christ, never by doing what the Law requires." (Galatians 2:16) In science, social advance, and personal living, beaten paths are for beaten men!

97

Tradition

When Bismarck was the Prussian ambassador to the court of Alexander II, in the early 1860's, he looked through a palace window and saw a sentry on duty in the middle of the vast lawn. He asked the Czar why the man was there. The Czar turned to an aide, inquired about the sentry, and found the aide did not know. The general in charge of the troops was called. When the question about the sentry's position was posed to him, he answered "I beg to inform his majesty that it is an ancient tradition." Bismarck, who was standing beside the Czar, asked, "What is the origin of this tradition?" The general admitted he didn't know. The Czar ordered, "Investigate this tradition and report the results!" They found that the sentry was posted there by an order put on the books eighty years before! One spring morning in 1780, Catherine the Great looked out on the lawn, saw the first flower thrusting above the frozen ground, and ordered a sentry to be posted to prevent anyone picking the flower. By 1860, the sentry on the lawn had become a tradition.

The word *tradition* comes from the Latin word "tradere," meaning to hand down. It refers to the handing down of beliefs, opinions, customs, and stories. Because a belief or custom is traditional does not guarantee it is true or right. In the Gospel according to John, for example, is an instance of an incorrect Church tradition. (21:23) In the second century, there was a group of eccentric Christians called Gnostics, who claimed to have a secret tradition different and superior to the church's ways. The ancient Church's response was to establish the Canon of Scripture, the list of documents recognized as the authoritative witness to the apostolic faith. To protect the church from erroneous unwritten traditions, St. Basil said: "It is a manifest falling from the faith . . . either to reject any point of these things that are written, or to bring in any of these things that are not written [in the Bible]."

98

Translate

A carpenter worked for a lumber company for forty years. After work each day, he'd carry home a few pieces of lumber. When he retired, he decided to build himself a house. When that was done, he still had lumber left, so he built a garage. Then he had a guilty conscience. Although he had never gone to church, he decided to go to confession. He told the priest, "Father, I worked for a lumber company for forty years and each day I carried home some lumber. From that I built a house." The priest said, "You know the Bible says, 'Thou shalt not steal'." The carpenter replied, "Father, I'm not finished. I had enough lumber left that I built a garage." The priest said, "That's bad, my son. You'll have to make a novena." The man rubbed his jaw and answered, "A novena, Father? I don't know. But if you have the plans, I'm sure I have enough lumber!"

Obviously, that man misunderstood the word novena. As much as I love the old Authorized King James' Version of the Bible, it, too, is filled with English words from the year 1611 (when it was published) that are misunderstood. Here are some examples, with the actual meaning in parentheses: Colossians 3:12 — "bowels" (compassion); Philippians 3:20 — "conversation" (citizenship); 1 Peter 3:2 — "conversation" (behavior); Acts 28:13 — "fetch a compass" (to sail round); 1 Thessalonians 4:15 — "prevent" (go ahead); 1 Corinthians 10:25 — "shambles" (meat market). Our English language is a living, changing reality. That's why I agree with Frederick Grant who said, "Biblical translation is an endless process." Our word *translate* comes from the Latin verb "transferre." That verb is formed from two Latin words: "trans" (across) and "ferre" (to carry). When the Bible is well translated, the meaning of the Hebrew and Greek words of the original text are carried over into English, so we can understand what the author meant. My favorite translations are *The New English Bible* and the *Good News Bible.*

99

Unjust Suffering

"If the Lord is really with us, why has all this happened to us?" asked Gideon in the Old Testament. (Judges 6:13) When Rabbi Harold Kushner's son, Aaron, was stricken with progeria (a rapid aging disease), the Rabbi investigated the traditional religious answers why bad things happened to good people. He discovered four answers he considered unsatisfactory to cover the problem: God is trouncing us (we're being punished for our sins); God is teaching us (we're being educated by these misfortunes); God is testing us (we're afflicted so God can learn how strong we are); God is transferring us (through terminal illness from this bitter world to a better one).

I believe there are five factors that point toward an answer to the question of *unjust suffering*. The events of Jesus' death focus them for us First, there is the power of moral *choice*. Outside his palace in Jerusalem the Roman governor, Pontius Pilate, asked the crowd: "Which one do you want me to set free for you? Jesus Barabbas or Jesus, called the Messiah?" (Matthew 27:27) Jesus suffered because of the choice people made. Second, there is the matter of *chance*. Inside Pilate's palace there was, by chance, a clever sadist who wove a crown from thorns to add to Jesus' suffering. Jesus recognized this ingredient of chance. In his parable about the Good Samaritan he said: "And by chance there came down a certain priest that way." (Luke 10:31). Third, the *charts* of nature's ways state that nails driven through living flesh and nerves cause pain. Jesus suffered because nature' laws apply to all. Fourth, there are *chains* of compassion that link one life to another. Mary, the mother of Jesus, suffered below the cross because love chained her there. Fifth, *charity*, divine love, moved Jesus to care for people, to volunteer to bear their burdens, and to become vulnerable to being hurt. The cross sums up the mystery of why bad things happen to good people, and calls us to ponder five words: choice, chance, charts, chains, and charity.

100

Untoward

In Arthur Miller's play *Death of a Salesman,* the central character is Willy Loman, a traveling salesman. Willy had chosen two superficial goals for his life: popularity and material success. He was intent on being a supersalesman. He wanted to be well liked. But his chosen goals were not fixed stars that gave his life stability; they were falling stars that disappeared and left him unsteady. His business began to slip. His fair-weather friends dropped away. The son, on whom he doted, caught him in a sordid affair in a cheap hotel, and despised him. Feeling lost and aimless, Willy committed suicide. In the last scene, there is only the mound of Willy's grave on a dark, bare stage. His wife and sons stand around it. There is a long silence, then one son says, "Poor guy, he had all the wrong dreams. Poor guy, he didn't know who he was." Miller's play puts a finger on the place where people today really hurt.

In our old King James' Version of the Bible there is one word that sums up the malady of modern man. It is the word *untoward.* When Simon Peter preached his first great sermon in Jerusalem, he pleaded with his listeners, "Save yourselves from this untoward generation." (Acts 2:40) The word *untoward* is a perfect translation of the Greek word "skolios," which means crooked, that is, not pointing toward anything, but meandering in all directions. An "untoward generation" is a generation which has no high aims, no overriding sense of high purpose. In Old English, the word toward is a complimentary adjective which describes someone who is obviously going somewhere. I agree with Dr. Viktor Frankl who says "the striving to find meaning in one's life is the primary motivational force in man." The absence of such a positive life purpose, says Frankl, leads to depression, addiction, and aggression.

For Further Reading

A Theological Word Book of the Bible. Edited by Alan Richardson. New York: Macmillan Company, 1955.

Barclay, William. *New Testament Words.* Philadelphia: Westminster Press, 1964.

Dictionary of Biblical Theology, Edited by Xavier Leon-Dufour, translated by P. Joseph Cahill, 2nd ed. New York; Seabury, 1973.

Epsy, Willard. O Thou Improper, Thou Uncommon Noun. New York: Clarkson N. Potter, Inc., 1978.

Evans, Bergen. *Comfortable Words.* New York: Random House, 1959.

Garrison, Webb B. *How It Started.* Nashville: Abingdon Press, 1972.

__________. *What's in a Word?* Nashville: Abingdon Press, 1954.

__________. *Why You Say It.* Nashville: Abingdon Press, 1955.

Newland-Smith, J. N. *Church Teaching for Church Children.* New York: Morehouse-Gorham, 1908, 1930.

Sorel, Nancy Caldwell. *Word People.* New York: American Heritage Press, 1970.

The Interpreter's Dictionary of the Bible. Four Volumes. Edited by George Arthur Buttrick. Nashville: Abingdon Press, 1962.

The Interpreter's Dictionary of the Bible. Supplementary Volume. Edited by Keith Crim. Nashville: Abingdon, 1976.

Turner, Nigel. *Christian Words.* Nashville: Thomas Nelson Publishers, 1981.

Vocabulary of the Bible. Edited by J. J. Von Allmen. London: Lutterworth Press, 1958.